Production, Equality and Participation in Rural China

M. Stiefel and W.F. Wertheim

The United Nations Research Institute for Social
Development is an autonomous United Nations activity, established for the purpose of conducting research into "problems
and policies of social development and relationships between
various types of social development and economic development
during different phases of economic growth". The studies of
the Institute are intended to contribute to (a) the work of
the United Nations Secretariat in the field of social policy,
social development planning and balanced economic and social
development; (b) regional planning institutes set up under
the auspices of the United Nations; (c) national institutes
in the field of economic and/or social development and planning.

Production, Equality and Participation in Rural China

M. Stiefel and W.F. Wertheim

United Nations Research Institute for Social Development, Palais des Nations, 1211 Geneva 10, Switzerland.

Zed Press, 57 Caledonian Road, London N1 9DN, U.K.

Production, Equality and Participation in Rural China was
first published jointly by UNRISD, Palais des Nations, 1211
Geneva 10, Switzerland, and Zed Press, 57 Caledonian Road,
London N1 9DN, U.K. in 1983.

Copyright © United Nations, 1983

Cover design by Jacque Solomons
Photographs in text and on cover by Matthias Stiefel,
    UNRISD, Geneva.
Maps in Annex III by H.M. van Groos, Department of
    Planning & Demography, University of Amsterdam.
Chinese translations in Annex II by Tsen Chung Lu,
    United Nations, Geneva.
Printed by The Pitman Press, Bath

British Library Cataloguing in Publication Data

Wertheim, W.
Production, equality and participation in rural China
1. Rural development—China
2. China—Economic conditions—1949-1976
3. China—Economic conditions—1976-
I. Title   II. Stiefel, M.
330.951'05   HC427.9

ISBN 0-86232-123-9

U.S. Distributor:
Biblio Distribution Center, 81 Adams Drive, Totowa,
New Jersey 07512, U.S.A.

CONTENTS

Page

PREFACE   i
FOREWORD   iii
INTRODUCTION   1

PART I: PRODUCTION AND REPRODUCTION
            A. Historical Outline   9
            B. Recent Developments and Present Trends   9
            C. Experiences during UNRISD Mission   20
                                                                           24

PART II: EQUALITY AND INEQUALITY
            A. Historical Outline   43
            B. Recent Developments and Present Trends   43
            C. Experiences during UNRISD Mission   56
                                                                           61

PART III: PARTICIPATION AND HIERARCHY
            A. Historical Outline   83
            B. Recent Developments and Present Trends   83
            C. Experiences during UNRISD Mission   95
                                                                           101

GENERAL CONCLUSIONS   127

APPENDIX I: Account of Local Level Meetings attended
                by Wertheim and Stiefel and their
                Interpreter, Mrs. Wang Huiying   139

APPENDIX II: Production Plan and Projections for 1979
                of Longmian Brigade (Tuyuan Commune)   151

APPENDIX III: Maps   159

Publications   169

Index   172

PREFACE

This monograph by Professor Wertheim and Mr. Stiefel looks at issues of production, equity and participation in contemporary rural China. It is based in part on a fairly short mission in 1979. A brief field mission, however, can yield significant insights if it is based upon a thorough knowledge of the literature, of the recent evolution of rural China and of similar issues in other Asian countries.

This was Professor Wertheim's fourth mission to China since 1957 and he was able to visit communes he had studied earlier. Moreover, he is one of the world's leading specialists on development issues in Indonesia. Mr. Stiefel is carrying on parallel research in Thailand and India. This highly informative and suggestive research report is an outcome of this mission.

The present report is published in connection with UNRISD's Popular Participation Programme. The Programme's aim is to help clarify and to make more useful operationally the idea of popular participation. The Programme consists of several research, action research and sub-debate projects. These are complementary and are linked together through a general debate on the theory and practice of participation. Monographs and occasional papers are published when the material is of broad interest and when the analyses are sufficiently advanced to warrant wide distribution. While this monograph is an Institute publication, the views expressed are those of the authors and do not necessarily reflect those of the Institute.

Although the present monograph is part of the Institute's Participation Programme, it is closely related to its research on food systems and society. In this connection, the reader might want to read it together with the Institute Food System Programme report on China, *The Family Rice Bowl* by Elisabeth Croll, which is being published simultaneously.

Solon L. Barraclough
Director
UNRISD

FOREWORD

The present volume is a welcome contribution to our knowledge on the cause of events and changes in politics and policies as they affect rural China during recent years. As is also the case in many other Third World countries, developing along either socialist or capitalist lines, there is a dearth of information on what is going on at the local level. Given the absence by and large of more intensive in-depth studies of social formations in the countryside based on research of longer duration and non-directed contacts with the peasantry, we shall have to make do for the time being with reports which are the outcome of short field trips made in close consultation with government agencies and other authorities. Does this automatically lead to a stage-managed representation of social reality and its dynamics? Or, in other words, is the outsider's view by necessity also a view from above only highlighting what those in power want us to see? Not if the authors combine, as is the case here, a critical understanding of past and present China with similar research experience in other Asian countries as well. Moreover they made clear that there was no interference in their schedule of visits. They were able to select the various localities on the basis of well-defined criteria and were in no way restricted in their freedom of movement - a basic research requirement.

There is a regrettable lack of Asian studies that are comparative in nature. Even two country analyses (China-Japan, China-India) are limited in number, let alone publications that focus on development processes in the region as a whole. Myrdal, however, published one of these 'studies with a wider scope' one-and-a-half decades ago. Ominously presented as a drama, the study summed up the state of affairs that existed in South and Southeast Asia around that time. But, no reference whatsoever was made to China in this voluminous work on the early post-colonial period. No explicit reasons were given for this omission, but presumably it was mainly because after the revolution, China deviated from the general pattern of Asian underdevelopment which was still prevalent at the beginning of the sixties. It was particularly in the following decade that the Chinese development strategy came to be regarded as a model that could successfully combine growth with distribution and popular participation. The latter were even held to be necessary, though not sufficient, conditions for an acceleration in the process of capital accumulation. Also, in the more careful reports which, instead of giving way to wishful thinking tried to adhere to sound principles of verification, setbacks and non-achievements could not easily be registered in a bureaucratic climate that took the realization of stated targets for granted while reacting adversely to the very mention of shortfalls, if not outrightly suppressing much undesired information. But indeed, as the authors point out, "failures" and "successes" are relative terms in a situation where communication flows are essentially one-sided and continue to be controlled from the top downwards. Apparently the growth in productivity has been lower than earlier proclaimed. Even the contention that at least the basic needs of all are met seems to have become doubtful now that we are told that a sizeable part of the total population, not less than one quarter, is said to live below the (non-defined) subsistence line. The same news item in a recent issue of the *Beijing Review* complains of collusion between party cadres and richer peasants leading to increasing local differentiation. One wonders if this emergent coalition, with the concomitant return once again of a betting-on-the-strong approach, is not the logical outcome of the liberalization of agricultural policies together with a shift in the balance of power at the local level.

One common type of comment to critical assessments like these, is to suggest that we should not really be surprised that the same mechanisms that explain the differential access to scarce resources and the non-participation of the rural poor in decision-making processes in other Asian countries, have also persisted in China. Thus a basic Asiatic pattern is

constructed, a structural-cultural configuration of long
standing, the main features of which are economic deprivation,
political dependency and social inequality. The overall
message is that China has more in common with South and
Southeast Asian societies than it cares to admit. Such a
facile view would not do justice to some of the major differences.
To begin with, preoccupation with short-term cycles and
glorifying present policies while repudiating those of the
immediate past, should be balanced by a historical perspective
that gives due weight to longer-term transformations, reflected
in the completion of the first revolutionary process in China
by the middle of the twentieth century. Furthermore, elsewhere
in Asia the soft states (a misconceived notion of earlier
government performance, particularly as far as the rural and
urban poor were concerned) have increasingly turned into harsh
regimes with a dominant ideology that comes close to social
darwinism. Disciplined action here is directed against the
non-propertied classes and has resulted in their economic
exploitation, political demobilization and social discrimination.
This is the type of negative lesson which, according to the
authors, China might draw from non-emancipatory policies in other
parts of Asia.

In their well-balanced argument, the authors on the one
hand express their reservations about some of the rural strategies which are currently being followed and, on the other hand,
warn against the tendency to condemn outright all that has
happened under the Cultural Revolution. Their findings go
against the black-and-white type of analysis which has become
so fashionable of late. Pointing to the positive sides of
the earlier state of affairs and to the negative sides of the
present situation, Wertheim and Stiefel have added a new
dimension to the China debate which will undoubtedly continue.

Both authors have an extensive knowledge of development issues in Asian countries. Professor Wertheim is a consultant to UNRISD's Participation Programme. Before his retirement he was Professor of Asian Sociology and History and Director of the Centre for South and Southeast Asian Studies at the University of Amsterdam. Mr. Stiefel is Director of UNRISD's Popular Participation Programme.

Jan Breman

Erasmus University (Rotterdam)
and Institute of Social Studies
(The Hague)
Member of the Central Core Group
of UNRISD's Participation
Programme

New Delhi
February 1982

Introduction

1.   The present study of rural strategies and participation in China is based in part on an exploratory mission carried out in 1979. The mission was undertaken on behalf of the United Nations Research Institute for Social Development (UNRISD), after its Board had approved a preliminary project proposal to study democratic centralism and the "mass line" in rural China, as part of UNRISD's Popular Participation Programme. The main purpose of the mission was to assess whether the necessary preconditions for a fruitful field research on people's participation in development, as defined in the project proposal, could be fulfilled.[1/] The task was particularly to evaluate whether an inquiry into the significance of popular participation as an element in Chinese rural strategy would produce relevant results and a better understanding of the functioning of basic democracy at the local level.

The mission was divided into two parts. During the first part W.F. Wertheim, acting as consultant for UNRISD, made preliminary explorations on behalf of its Participation Programme and attempted to obtain an orientation of a more general nature on the issue of participation in China. He had discussions with experts in several fields and made visits to six people's communes close to major cities and towns and to one state farm, most of which he had already visited during earlier trips to China and on which he had detailed information.

The first part of the mission provided the research team with a general impression of the present situation as well as official views and attitudes and served as a preparation for the second part, which Wertheim carried out with Matthias Stiefel,

---

[1/] Research proposal: *Democratic Centralism and the Mass Line in Rural China*, UNRISD/79/C.24, June 1979.

in charge of the Participation Programme. During this second part we made preliminary field research in three people's communes in Guangdong, Hubei and Sichuan provinces, and investigated possibilities for research and cooperation at the local and central levels. The mission was concluded with a stay in Beijing, which served to finalize the preparations for later research projects to be proposed by UNRISD.

2. A number of factors led to the choice of the People's Republic of China as a case to be studied under the UNRISD Participation Programme.[1]

Previous UNRISD studies, such as those on cooperatives and on the socio-economic impact of the Green Revolution, have shown that prevailing social, economic and political structures and relations in most Third World countries are hardly favourable to the participation of the poor majority in the definition and implementation of rural policies. The removal, or the relative neutralization of the impact of such *structures* or *outer obstacles* to participation as we may call them, seems a basic precondition to increased popular participation. At a relatively early stage of its development China eliminated many of these outer obstacles through a radical social revolution based on large-scale active participation of the rural poor and, during the past three decades, development efforts have apparently been based on a high level of people's participation in the definition and implementation of policies. Compared to that of other Third World

---

[1] For a discussion of the theoretical and conceptual framework of the Participation Programme, see Andrew Pearse and Matthias Stiefel, *Inquiry into Participation*, UNRISD/79/C.14, Geneva, May 1979. This document states that the central issue of popular participation has to do with power, exercised by some people over other people and by some classes over other classes. The kinds of participation considered in this inquiry are organized efforts to increase control over resources and regulative institutions in given local situations on the part of or on behalf of groups and movements of those hitherto largely excluded from such control.

countries, this experience in participatory development, based on new democratic forms and procedures, seems to have been remarkably successful in improving and securing livelihood and basic services for the majority of its citizens. However, it has also brought out in increasingly sharp terms what seem to be the *inner limits* of people's participation: constraints to forms of direct democracy associated with the need for efficiency and with contradictions between local and supra-local interests, individual and collective goals. The study of this Chinese experience of participation seemed not only interesting from a historical point of view, but interesting at least as much as a way to investigate the present strategies of rural development initiated since 1977 and apparently aiming at basic socio-economic changes.

In our discussions and field investigations, however, we went deliberately beyond an inquiry into questions related directly to people's participation, study of which requires first a comprehensive understanding of the overall rural strategy and development process as well as of key issues and problems at different stages of decision-making. Our questions thus covered a wide spectrum of issues dealing as well with problems of agricultural mechanization, equality and inequality issues, the impact of the Cultural Revolution, rural industries, minority problems as well as questions more directly related to participation such as decision-making processes at the local level, the relative role of the party, the administration and the mass organizations, etc.

3.   To study rural problems and strategies in China today requires a knowledge and understanding of their background. Both of us are thoroughly acquainted with rural problems and developments in several countries of South and Southeast Asia. Whereas Wertheim has all his life been mainly concerned with Indonesia, he has also supervised the field research in India and the Philippines of several of his students from the University of Amsterdam. Stiefel has concentrated his studies principally on

the countries of continental Southeast Asia (Burma, Thailand,
Laos, Cambodia and Vietnam), in addition to gathering general
information on the large countries of South Asia.   Moreover, for
Wertheim this was his fourth visit to China; during his earlier
visits (in 1957, 1964 and 1970/71) he had paid specific attention
to rural developments, which enabled us to view present situations,
strategies and developments in a historical perspective.
Stiefel's second visit to Beijing in November 1980, to continue
the discussions with the Chinese Academy of Social Sciences on
scientific collaboration with UNRISD, allowed him to discuss again
a number of issues studied during the joint mission with Wertheim
in 1979.

     Of course, researchers have to take into account China's
size and its enormous regional differences.   Though in our choice
of localities we attempted to select places more or less
representative of the average level of development in China (and
thus remote from large cities), situated at a great distance from
each other, and with widely differing geographic, topographic and
climatic characteristics, they are all situated in preponderantly
rice-growing areas in the Southern and Central parts of China.
Our preference for rice-growing regions can be explained by our
general acquaintance with societies where rice cultivation is
dominant, which made it easier for us to assess both the problems
and the achievements of the Chinese people in comparison with
countries south of the Himalayas.   This selection implies that we
feel obliged to warn the reader that our analysis cannot automatically be applied to agricultural regions in Northern China,
with very different agricultural patterns and widely divergent
geographic and climatic conditions.   Nevertheless, we believe
that certain main trends observed concerning the problems of
change and adaptation to new general policies, as well as
decision-making processes at the local level are to a certain
extent applicable to all of China.

4.   The possibilities of fulfilling our mission depended in the
first place on the facilities made available by the Chinese
authorities.   In our case, our travel was arranged by the Chinese
People's Friendship Association with Foreign Countries in Beijing,
which had agreed to act as an official counterpart.   The
Association did its utmost to facilitate and organize a trip that
was clearly beyond its normal duties and tasks and was extremely
helpful in fulfilling practically all the wishes we had expressed
in order to make our mission as fruitful as possible.

     We had planned to do research in people's communes that
would be much nearer to the average level of rural China than
those near the cities familiar to tourists and foreign delegations.
During the first part of the mission, as already indicated,
Wertheim had found the opportunity to revisit several places near
big cities which he already knew from his earlier visits; also, in
the course of the second part of our mission, we paid casual
visits to places that Wertheim already had visited before, and
which could be considered more or less as model communes, situated
on our way to or from faraway districts (*Dali* commune near
Guangzhou, and *Liuji* commune in Xinzhou district, Hubei province).

     But our intention was to visit mainly those places that,
during his earlier visit to ten people's communes and two state
farms in 1964, Wertheim had identified as units definitely below
the level of development generally described in accounts by
foreign visitors.   The two communes selected on this basis were
Tuyuan commune (Xinhui district, Guangdong province), and
Liangjiafan subcommune (*Baiguo* commune, Macheng district, Hubei
province), both situated at a far distance from any large urban
centre.

     In addition we expressed the wish to do research in a
people's commune in a mountainous region of Sichuan province,
which has never before been visited by foreign researchers.
Though the authorities have more than once suggested, both in
Sichuan province and elsewhere, that we should visit also a more
prosperous commune in the same district or province, in addition

to the poorer type of commune proposed by us, we were able to convince them that since Wertheim had already visited several prosperous communes during the first part of the mission, it would be much more useful for our purpose to stay for a longer period in one place and to penetrate more deeply into the problems of one single collective unit. The Friendship Association not only showed full understanding of our wishes, but its representative - who was at the same time our escort during the whole trip and an excellent interpreter - also succeeded in persuading the provincial branches of the Association and the local authorities to arrange a programme in accordance with our wishes. *Longchi*, the people's commune selected in Sichuan for us, was the type of commune we had proposed: high in the mountains and far from any urban centre, in the Emei district. The general curiosity with which we were received by the inhabitants, especially the children, confirmed that the three places where we concentrated our research had hardly ever been visited by foreigners, at least by visitors from the West.

District officials as well as leaders of people's communes and subordinate collective units extended all kinds of facilities to us, some of them quite unusual. During our stay in China we became convinced that the type of social science research we wanted to undertake has only become possible very recently, and that the opportunities offered to us in terms of freedom of investigation, random interviewing, access to statistics, etc. most probably would not have been available in an earlier period. We were also struck by the openness with which all those with whom we came into contact were prepared to discuss all kinds of problems, of the past as well as of the present period.

One of the crucial questions to which we tried to find an answer was whether the issue of popular participation could be studied only in a historical context, in an atmosphere more or less disengaged from recent ideological discussions, or whether the research would also be allowed to encompass the more recent

6

period, starting with the Cultural Revolution.[1] We found that
the latter type of research is not only possible but necessary to
investigate actual degrees and modalities of people's participation in decision-making, and that no strong inhibitions frustrate
research on what happened in recent periods.

Finally, a few remarks on the linguistic aspect of our
research: Wertheim is able to read Chinese, if only with the help
of a dictionary; but since in Putonghua speech he is far from
fluent, an interpreter (mostly in French, but occasionally in
English or German) was always needed. Moreover, for local
dialects, particularly in Guangdong province, the assistance of
interpreters well acquainted with the regional language was
necessary for discussions with the local population, which, unlike
the cadres, was often unable to speak or understand Putonghua,
since interpreters from North or Central China also had great
difficulty in conversing with the local people.

The present report is divided into three main parts, dealing
respectively with questions of "Production and Reproduction" (Part
I), "Equality and Inequality" (Part II), and "Participation and
Hierarchy" (Part III). We have concentrated most of our findings
in these three chapters; however, they do not contain the results
of less thorough investigations we made on industrial management,
minority questions and the state of social sciences in China. An
account of two local level meetings we attended, which gave us a
vivid picture of *de facto* participation of the peasants in
agricultural policy-making at the grassroots level, is annexed.

We would like to acknowledge our deep appreciation of the
Chinese People's Friendship Association with Foreign Countries,
without which our field trip would not have been possible, but
most of all we would like to thank the peasants, workers and cadres
at the local levels who so willingly spent their time to answer our

---

[1] See the research proposal on *Democratic Centralism and the Mass
Line in Rural China*, UNRISD/79/C.24, June 1979.

7

questions in long and often tedious interviews and discussions
that lasted sometimes until late into the night. We would also
like to thank central authorities in Beijing, as well as the
office of the United Nations Development Programme (UNDP) there,
for the help, advice and assistance offered in the course of our
mission.

—————————oOo—————————

PART I

PRODUCTION AND REPRODUCTION

Since Mao Zedong's death, Chinese policy has been determined by the magic catchphrase "the four modernizations". The four fields are: agricultural production; industrial production; military defence; and science and technology. The Chinese leaders aspire to such a rapid progress that their country will catch up with the Western industrialized countries within a relatively short time. But their efforts are meeting serious obstacles, of which they are gradually becoming aware.

In the present section we concentrate mainly on one aspect - albeit a basic one - of these obstacles: the manpower and under-employment issue. China as a whole belongs to the over-populated Asian world, and this has serious implications that the Chinese leadership has come to realize and admit only very recently.

A. Historical Outline

When Wertheim visited China for the first time in 1957, he was invited to read a lecture at the Academy of Sciences (Academia Sinica) in Beijing. His subject was over-population on Java, the main island of Indonesia. Before travelling to China, he had been teaching there and conducting research in the countryside for one year, as visiting professor at the Faculty of Agriculture in Bogor, which at that time formed part of the University of Indonesia.

The session was presided over by Mr. Ma Yinchu, a well-known economist who was then Rector at Beijing University (*Beida*). In some of his recent publications, Professor Ma had drawn attention to the population problem in China and, among other solutions, he had proposed family planning, which at that time was considered by some a "neo-Malthusian" deviation from Marxist principles. According to classical Marxist theory, over-population as defined around 1800 by Malthus cannot exist. If part of the world population goes hungry, this is not caused by their numbers, but because the capitalist mode of production is not capable of fully utilizing productive forces and accounts for serious maldistribution of available goods. Marxism, as still interpreted by Soviet leaders in the fifties, denied any justification for the use of "over-population" as a scientific term; instead of limitation of births, what mattered was increasing production in such a way that sufficient food would become available to everybody. Under a capitalist system, which advocated curbs on production as well as on reproduction, this aim could never be achieved.

The problem that most interested Wertheim during his first visit to China was to study how the Chinese tried to develop the rural economy in those very densely populated areas where irrigated rice farming predominated. It was in these regions that, according to the expression coined by the American agronomist F.H. King, "the farmers of forty centuries" were to be found.[1] According to King, the countries of East Asia (China, Korea and Japan) long before the Christian era had developed agricultural techniques that made it possible to maintain high population densities in rural areas with a sedentary type of agriculture far beyond anything achieved in the Western world. But at present, with stable birth rates and falling death rates, these countries are being confronted with the problem of achieving modern economic development under conditions of intensive agriculture and high population densities. The same problem was haunting the island of Java, and no solution has yet been found there; it also affected Indo-China, where it has been studied by the French

---

[1] F.H. King, *Farmers of Forty Centuries, or permanent agriculture in China, Korea and Japan*, Madison, 1911.

geographer Pierre Gourou.[1]

At the time of Wertheim's visit, in 1957, tractors had already been introduced in the People's Republic of China, following the example of the Soviet Union; they were owned by cooperatives or state farms, mostly in the northern regions of China. But it was clear that for the southern regions, where irrigated rice farming predominates, tractors were no solution. At that time no tractor suitable for wet rice fields had yet been developed. But the main reason was that premature mechanization would create a serious underemployment problem in very densely populated areas.

It was evident that at that time urban industry could not be developed in China at a sufficiently rapid pace that the natural population increase could be more or less absorbed, as had been possible in Japan during the early decades of this century at a time when the death rate was falling more gradually. One could, therefore, understand quite well why Mao Zedong had insisted that China had "to learn to walk on two legs". He meant that agricultural mechanization, and the introduction of modern machinery in general, had to be combined with a development of the traditional labour-intensive technologies, which China would still need for a long time to come.

In addition, at that time much effort was devoted to re-forestation of the hillsides, denuded in the course of centuries. Abolition of landlordism had made this strategy possible since before the revolution in several regions the hillsides had been owned by the gentry, who left considerable parts of them all but uncultivated (as, for example, the vast hillsides covered with cemeteries that we saw in the southern Guangdong province). On this problem of denuded hillsides, so much in contrast with the intensively cultivated river valleys, Pierre Gourou had written an

---

[1] Pierre Gourou, *Utilisation du sol en Indochine française*, Paris, 1940. See also, J.H. Boeke, *The Interests of the Voiceless Far East: Introduction to Oriental Economics*, Leiden, 1948.

The premature replacement of traditional labour-intensive technologies through rapid mechanisation could lead to serious underemployment problems in densely-populated areas. (Construction work in Guangzhou)

important article shortly before Liberation[1]; reforestation was precisely one of the measures the author had advocated, and now the Chinese, apparently without being aware of it, were following his advice. However, it was evident that, although reforestation would increase the total cultivable area of China, it would far from suffice to solve the over-population problem in the plains and river valleys earmarked for wet-rice cultivation.

In the following years dramatic developments took place in China, such as the formation of people's communes and the Great Leap Forward, followed by the three years (1959-1961) of natural catastrophes (droughts and inundations). Professor Ma Yinchu had been dismissed as Rector of Beijing University during the Great Leap Forward, not because of his age (he was already 76 years old) but owing to his ideas. These were considered as being "neo-Malthusian", which brought about his fall from grace.

In the summer of 1964, when Wertheim visited China for the second time, ideas on the population issue in China had not yet come to maturity. The natural calamities of 1959 to 1961 had not led to a thorough reappraisal of views on population growth. In actual practice family planning was now being propagated, but the arguments for birth control had nothing to do with Malthusian ideas. The reason why a delay of marriages and spacing between births were advocated was rather to be found in concern for the health of the mother and the well-being of the family. Particularly since the Great Leap Forward women had played an increasing role in agricultural production, and in the interests of the family it became essential that the mother should not be encumbered by the care of a large number of toddlers, which would cost the family valuable work points.

In his work, *From Malthus to Mao Zedong*[2], the French

---

[1] Pierre Gourou, "Notes on China's Unused Uplands", *Pacific Affairs*, Vol.20, 1948, pp.227 ff.

[2] Alfred Sauvy, *De Malthus à Mao Tsé-toung*, Paris, 1958.

demographer Alfred Sauvy has demonstrated the significant *practical* contribution of the Chinese leaders in promoting birth control. But the Chinese Marxists had, at that time, not yet admitted the existence of an over-population problem as such. Their main problem was to find a solution for an optimal utilization of their greatest wealth: abundance of manpower.

About 1962, after the three catastrophic years, the Chinese leaders realized that economic strategy had to be thoroughly revised. It had become clear that a solution for the problem of excessive manpower should not be sought, first and foremost, through accelerated urban industrial development (the strategy of the fifties), which required significant capital investment. The main accent was to be on a still-increasing intensification of traditional agricultural techniques. Full use of available manpower had to be stressed, and efforts concentrated in the first place on those regions where, owing to a good irrigation system, the marginal value of added manpower would be highest. The essence of this new strategy was to succeed in augmenting the number of annual harvests so as to create an additional demand for manpower.

Concentrating on well-irrigated areas (fields with "stable high yields") did not preclude a gradual introduction of agricultural machinery. In many cases the use of threshing machinery or tractors accelerated the harvesting or ploughing process and thus reduced the interval between two successive crops. In this way, the number of crops per year could be raised; if this happened, partial mechanization did not reduce but increased the demand for (purely manual) manpower.

The new strategy also affected Chinese rural-urban migration policies. Whereas in most Third World countries there is a large-scale exodus of impoverished peasants and unemployed landless labourers to urban areas, in China a migration stream from the countryside to the large cities has been deliberately curbed. The stream has been in the other direction: educated young people (e.g. secondary school graduates from the towns) were called upon

14

to move to the rural areas to put their acquired knowledge and training at the service of people's communes. The underlying idea was not only to prevent a serious unemployment problem in urban societies, but also to strengthen rural manpower, not only quantitatively but also qualitatively. At the same time, efforts were made to improve the level of agricultural knowledge and technological training of the peasantry by improving school education and organizing all kinds of courses, particularly during the slack winter season. At the same time this season could be used for collective construction of hydraulic and other infrastructural works, as well as for collecting manure from the bottom of canals, rivers and ponds.

In short, the rural-urban migration policies as conceived by the Chinese leadership could serve to reduce the gap in social status between urban and rural people, and between intellectuals and manual workers.

This strategy of forced intensification of the agricultural labour process has allowed the Chinese basically to produce and distribute enough food for a minimum diet for all in their country[1] - a problem that, despite attempted green revolutions

---

[1] According to Peter Nolan and Gordon White, "the main advances have come in pork and sugar-cane". As far as grain production is concerned, China has been able to keep up with a high rate of population growth; the authors write: "Simply to keep up with a population growth of 2% or more is a major achievement for the farm sector of any country".

Per capita output in kgs.

	1952	1957	1978
Grain (incl. soybeans)	285.00	304.00	318.00
Sugar-cane	12.40	16.20	22.00
Pigs (in the pen)	0.16	0.22	0.31

However, the most outstanding achievement of the Chinese was in the realm of food distribution, a high portion of grain for consumption being "distributed 'according to need' on a per capita basis usually differentiated by age". ("Distribution and Development in China", *Bulletin of Concerned Asian Scholars*, China Special No.2, 1981, 2 ff.)

Collectivization of ownership and exploitation of land had allowed the more rational and planned use of available manpower and the development of intensive agriculture. (Workteam on Longmian Brigade, Tuyuan commune, Guangdong.)

and "basic needs" strategies, still haunts so many Third World countries.   The main stress was not put on a limitation of natural population increase, but on the increase of food production, starting from the Marxist principle according to which man is not only a consumer but also a producer.

However, raising food production was not pursued in the first place by raising per capita productivity, which would require fast mechanization.   The Chinese strategy consisted mainly of raising productivity by increasing output per land unit. This was essentially the traditional way of meeting population pressure - by increasing the number of annual crops.   However, the socialist system, by introducing collective ownership and exploitation of land, had allowed available manpower to be used in a more rational and planned manner.   The formation of people's communes, in particular, had enabled the Chinese to develop intensive agriculture at a much faster rate than before Liberation.

By a full use of rural labour and a steady increase of output per land unit, the Chinese communists have created a model for the more densely-populated regions of the Third World, which are to be found mainly in South and Southeast Asia.   However, it should be borne in mind that the application of this model presupposes a social revolution comparable with China's.

We should note that this solution of the over-population problem could be applied only for the first phase of economic development.   Inevitably, raising per capita productivity would have to be considered at a later stage in the development process. The Chinese themselves called the strategy pursued after the failure of the Great Leap Forward: *adopting agriculture as the foundation of the national economy, with industry as the leading factor*.   This implied that though the role of industry was temporarily played down and agriculture was given absolute priority, possibilities for future growth would have to be determined by the level of industrial capacity.   Mechanization of agriculture remained on the agenda though the pace of its development, it was now realized, had to take account of the need to maintain full employment.

Nevertheless, for a visitor in 1964 certain contradictions were apparent even then. When leaders of people's communes were asked if they experienced a surplus of manpower, the stereotyped reply would come: "On the contrary, we suffer from a shortage of manpower". Heavy demand for unskilled labour during the peak seasons, for transplanting or harvesting, was in their minds. However, if they were asked what they intended to do with their redundant manpower as soon as mechanization actually got under way, it became clear that this problem had not yet been seriously considered. Evidently, they had taken the cue of a pretended manpower shortage from the official party line; and there, too, long-term planning was obviously largely lacking.

After his second visit to China, in 1964, Wertheim expected that, since the Chinese had basically solved the food problem, they would soon feel impelled to switch over to a type of economic development more similar to the Soviet pattern, with greater stress on mechanization and industrial development.[1] However, by the time of his third visit in the winter of 1970/1971, such a switch had not occurred. On the contrary, the rural strategy adopted during the Cultural Revolution of 1966/1967 could rather be interpreted as a continuation of the early sixties' stress on intensive agriculture.

There had been, of course, some striking developments. For example, birth control had progressed a lot since 1964; consequently, for several years the population growth rate had slowed appreciably, particularly in the urban centres and in people's communes in the neighbourhood of cities. In the rural areas also a considerable drop in the growth rate had been achieved, mainly

---

[1] W.F. Wertheim, "La Chine est-elle sous-peuplée? Production agricole et main-d'oeuvre rurale", *Population*, Vol.20, 1965, pp. 477 ff.

18

by a significant innovation introduced during the Cultural Revolution: barefoot doctors, who, within the people's communes, were active in propagating family planning and in explaining birth-prevention techniques.[1]

However, there had been hardly any basic change in the rural strategy. Stress was still being laid on grain production, and on national and regional autarchy in food, in accordance with Mao's directive "to take grain as the main link in the national economy". Full utilization of available rural manpower on behalf of intensive agriculture was still the pattern. It could even be argued that the Cultural Revolution had reinforced the tendency to anticipate a long period to come in which a sober and Spartan way of life would be exemplary for the whole population. The pattern for rural development was set by the famous *Dazhai* brigade in Northern China, where, in spite of highly unfavourable natural conditions, great successes had been achieved with traditional means and implements, owing to a huge collective human effort.

The example of a sober and rustic way of life also had to be followed by large numbers of young graduates from secondary schools, who were urged to "go up to the mountains and down to the villages" and to settle forever in the countryside.[2] In addition, urban cadres were periodically sent to the countryside to participate in manual labour (for example in the "7 May cadre schools"). As well as being attempts to prevent serious unemployment in the towns, such measures were also intended to eradicate élitist attitudes among urban people, especially the younger ones, who often seemed more interested in making a career than in serving the people.

---

[1] Cf. F.P. Lisowski, "The Emergence and Development of the Barefoot Doctor in China", *Journal of the Japanese Society of Medical History*, Vol.25, 1979, pp.339 ff.

[2] Cf. Thomas P. Bernstein, *Up to the Mountains and Down to the Villages: The Transfer of Urban Youth from Urban to Rural China*, New Haven/London, 1977.

Diversification of the rural economy was still on the programme, and Mao's directive that, next to agriculture, arbori-
culture, livestock raising, rural industry and fisheries also had
to be developed (*nong-lin-mu-fu-yu*) was still regularly invoked.
In several places new initiatives could be observed and irrigation
works were being completed.   Agricultural mechanization was
making headway; consequently, there was again reason to enquire
what they were going to do about the surplus of manpower they
could expect as soon as mechanization assumed bigger proportions
and the danger of underemployment came to the fore.   Evidently,
however, long-term planning at that time was not in vogue in
China: the usual reply was that, as soon as the problem presented
itself, a solution would be sought "in accordance with the wants
of the people".[1]

B. Recent Developments and Present Trends

It is evident that in the theoretical approach to population
problems great changes have occurred.   Symbolic of these changes
is that during our mission Professor Ma Yinchu, now 98 years old,
was rehabilitated.   He has been able to enjoy the ultimate
victory of his ideas and, in recognition, received nomination as
Honorary Rector of Beijing University.

Henceforth, birth control is no longer advocated exclusively
as a measure to promote the welfare and health of individual
families; it is considered first and foremost as an indispensable
precondition for realizing the "four modernizations", so ardently
pursued by the present leadership.   The reasons for the new
strategy can therefore be labelled as purely "neo-Malthusian".

---

[1] W.F. Wertheim, "Rainbow Bridge Commune Revisited", *Eastern
Horizon*, Vol.10, No.6, 1971 pp.7 ff. and Vol.11, No.1, 1972,
pp.31 ff.

However, it would be an error to consider this new strategy as a complete break with the past. Throughout the seventies, family planning has been strongly promoted, and birth rates have been brought down to a level that is remarkably low if compared with the results achieved in most agrarian countries of the Third World (China's present average natural increase is calculated as 12 per thousand[1/]). At the time of Chairman Mao's death, the Chinese leadership was fully aware of these successes, achieved by steady and intensive propaganda. In a publication of October 26, 1976, issued by the People's Health Press the successes of the large-scale campaign were expounded even though "the great victory won by crushing of the anti-Party clique of Wang Hongwen, Zhang Chunqiao, Jiang Ching and Yao Wenyuan" was duly applauded:

> "Since the Great Proletarian Cultural Revolution, under the brilliant guidance of Chairman Mao's revolutionary line, family planning work has achieved great results. The broad masses have continually increased their consciousness of carrying out delayed marriage and family planning for the revolution... Late romances and delayed marriages have become the fashion among the young people."

About the way these results were obtained the following lines are indicative:

> "In the work of initiating family planning all localities have greatly stressed propaganda work and have compiled large quantities of source materials to propagate the Party's family planning policies."

The family planning message was also pursued "in literature and the arts which have been very popular among the worker - peasant - soldier masses."[2/]

[1/] There is reason seriously to doubt the correctness of this estimate; Professor Gilbert Etienne, for example, thinks that the actual rate of increase is still considerably higher.

[2/] *Jihua shengyu wenyi xuanchuan cailiao huibian*, Beijing, 1976, translation in *Chinese Sociology and Anthropology*, Vol.11, 1979, Nos.3/4, pp.3-5.

The question therefore arises why, despite the successes achieved by popular education and propaganda, birth control is now being pursued through much more draconian measures, with material incentives and sanctions. We will return to this question in due course; for the moment, it seems important to point out that the new population policies seem to be closely related to a new rural development strategy.

As we have seen, during the fifties Mao had stated that the Chinese should learn to "walk on two legs", that is, to maintain traditional techniques and develop these further, as well as introducing modern industrial technology and agricultural mechanization. During the Cultural Revolution this stress on traditional techniques was even reinforced by the choice of Dazhai brigade in Shanxi province (Xiyang district) as a model for Chinese agriculture. For some time Dazhai seems to have been purposely kept intact as a showcase to demonstrate how self-sufficiency could be achieved with *primitive* techniques and self-reliance. But after 1970 here, too, agricultural mechanization went ahead, and it was not without symbolic significance that Dazhai was selected as the venue for a big conference organized in 1975 to discuss means of accelerating agrarian mechanization. (The conference, where Hua Guofeng, at that time not yet so prominent, set the key note, was later continued in Beijing.)

After Mao's death the stress on rural mechanization was considerably reinforced. Concurrently, industrial development, which had been slowed down since the early sixties, has been tackled during the past few years with renewed energy. It is this increased accent on the "four modernizations" that also directly influences the attitudes of leaders at both central and local level to the population problem. For it is clear that whenever the introduction of modern technology implies a reduction of employment, the existence of a huge reservoir of manpower acts as a brake on modernization efforts.

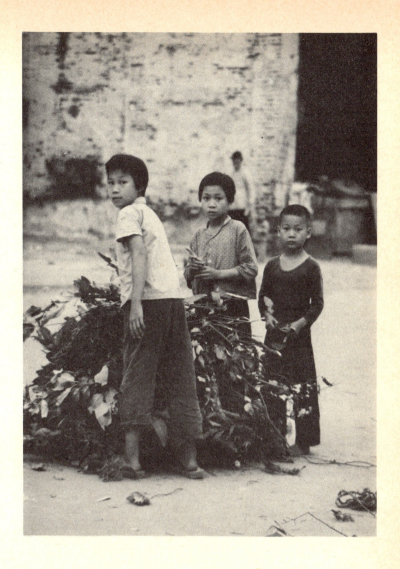

Birth control is seen as an indispensable precondition for realizing the "four modernizations" in a new phase of economic development where stress is no longer laid on increasing productivity per land unit but on increasing per capita productivity. (Children in Xinhui, Guangdong.)

It is apparent, therefore, that long-term perspectives are also currently being taken into account. It is also indisputable that solutions as applied in China to tackle the problem of rural over-population in the first phase of economic development no longer function optimally; also, that this has been the case for a number of years. There was evidently a ceiling above which further intensification of traditional agricultural practices could no longer absorb all the available, and gradually growing, manpower. Mechanization of agricultural techniques necessarily leads to a situation where a way out has to be found for the workers who have become redundant in traditional agriculture. The "homeopathic" solution of adding ever more people to already densely populated localities cannot be expanded indefinitely.

At present China is confronted with the problem of how to make a transition toward a second phase of economic development in which stress will no longer be laid on productivity per land unit but on *per capita* productivity, without jeopardizing the principal achievements of three decades.

C. Experiences during UNRISD Mission

Local research that we were able to carry out during our mission has convinced us that the transition to the second phase, as imagined and attempted by the present Chinese leaders, raises many doubts and contradictions. The main difficulty is that the new solutions are being presented as complete and absolute reversals of strategies pursued since the start of the Cultural Revolution, without admission that solutions found in previous decades were quite logical in view of conditions at that time. The image of the Cultural Revolution officially presented is all but completely negative. There are often references to "ten lost years"[1], and in several fields attempts are being made to force

---

[1] Deng Xiaoping, in his address to 10,000 cadres in Beijing on 16 January 1980 (a curious counterpart of Mao's address to 10,000 cadres in 1962!) even complained of *twenty* "lost years".

the pace, as though "lost time" should be recovered.   It is precisely this undue haste and negation of a certain continuity with
the past that could jeopardize the ultimate success of solutions
to initiate the second phase.   The new leadership tendency to set
fixed targets to be accomplished within ten, twenty or even more
years, and based on calculations carried out by experts, has
introduced an element of precipitation difficult to reconcile with
the principle of consulting the masses, so far considered a basic
factor of Chinese policies.

     In Shanghai, Wertheim met a group of demographers and socio-
logists who were working in institutes related to the Academy of
Social Sciences in Shanghai.   They briefed him on the specific
birth control measures taken in Shanghai municipality, and on the
demographic situation in China in general, and in Shanghai in particular.   The severe measures taken to reduce the natural increase
in population to zero within a rather short time and to limit
family size to one child per couple by incentives combined with
sanctions, are seen as a *temporary* strategy.   One of the main
reasons for a drastic limitation of procreation, so much in contrast with the more gradual method of mass education adopted
during earlier decades, appears to be a fear of the consequences
of a reproduction of the post-liberation baby boom one generation
later.   "After the anticipated new birth wave we can relax a bit",
they said.   "Then things will become easier".   These experts did
not seem aware of the danger that a rapidly ageing population could
result from drastic limitation of the number of children per
couple, and that such a policy would not in the long run improve
the numerical proportion between active population and dependants.
Indeed, old dependants would in the future present a new burden on
the active population just as an excessive number of children now.

     However, the experts were prepared to admit that the main
issue is not population numbers as such, but the relationship
between manpower and employment.   They also acknowledged that too
speedy mechanization of agriculture would create a serious unemployment problem.   Peasants in the neighbourhood of Shanghai,
they said, do not seem to be much interested in mechanization in

25

view of their surplus of manpower.   They prefer to do the transplanting of rice by hand rather than getting machinery for it: it
would cost them work points!

In Shanghai the seriousness of the unemployment problem was
brought home to the authorities by hundreds of thousands of young
people returning from the countryside.   Evidently, many of them
who during the Cultural Revolution had gone "up to the mountains
and down to the villages"[1] were not satisfied with their living
conditions and prospects for the future;   also the rural people
were very reserved in welcoming these "useless" young people.
When the authorities announced that those who had moved during the
past decades were allowed to return to their home town, large
numbers did so.   In Shanghai, the number of those who returned
during the first half of 1979, according to the experts from
Shanghai, was approximately 600,000.   Providing these young people
with employment has proved very difficult and there have been
vagabondage and crime, though on a limited scale, among those who
had problems finding suitable work, or experienced problems in
adjusting to their new environment.

At present, the Chinese seem to admit that allowing youth to
return all at once was risky and unwise;   they had overrated the
number of new employment opportunities in the wake of "the four
modernizations".   A gradual solution would have been preferable.

Another aspect of employment problems was encountered on a
visit to a chemical fertilizer factory (ureum) near Nanjing.   The
blueprints and machinery for the plant had been provided by
foreign companies, in accordance with the conceptions of advanced
foreign technology.   Consequently, the plant was nearly fully
automated.   In a country where a surplus of manpower is one of
the greatest social and economic problems, this does not seem the
most appropriate solution, although in the given case there may
have been particular reasons why this type of industry was intro-

---

[1] See Bernstein, *op.cit.*

duced.

In people's communes visited by Wertheim during the earlier phase of the mission and in those where we were able to stay for a longer period it was striking that even at the commune level the leaders had now become aware of the existence of an over-population problem. Repeatedly the commune leaders mentioned population density, without our asking about it; locally we were told in a worried tone, it was about one *mou* (1/15 ha.) of culti-vable land or even less per person.[1] During his earlier visits, Wertheim's questions about local population densities had not evoked any reaction. Evidently, at *that* time it was not realized that later this proportion of people to land could become a serious problem. The Chinese *now* quote this proportion in order to argue that one cannot merely stress grain production as "the main link of the national economy". Diversification of local production is inevitable, and development of rural industry has to go hand in hand with the development of urban industry.

Two of the localities in the Chinese interior, where we spent a number of days, provided new insights to the population issue.

---

[1] Population densities in some of the communes visited were as follows:

	mou cultivated land/inhabitant
– Macheng district:	0.90
– Liangjiafan subcommune:	0.75
– Liangzhu commune (near Hangzhou), Zhejiang province:	0.93
– Hongjiao commune, near Shanghai:	0.71
– Tuyuan commune, Xinhui district:	0.99
– Evergreen commune, near Suzhou:	0.68
– Dongbeiwang commune, near Beijing:	1.32

See also W.F. Wertheim, "Toujours plus de travailleurs par *mou* de terre", in Marthe Engelborghs-Bertels (Ed.), *La commune populaire chinoise*, Brussels, 1978.

(1) Liangjiafan

In 1964, when Wertheim visited *Liangjiafan people's commune*, in *Macheng district* (ca. 140 km. northeast from Wuhan) he had found an interesting experiment under way. He was met by Mr. Peng Sihan, at that time one of the directors of the commune. He was a remarkable person. Before liberation, he had been a farmhand. During the fifties, he had proposed to introduce two crops of rice in the commune. The old peasants opposed the idea, asserting that it was impossible to have two crops of rice so far north of Chang Jiang (Yangtse) river; frost would destroy the late crop before it could be harvested. If a second crop was possible, they said, their ancestors would certainly have introduced it!

With the assistance of a group of young peasants, Mr. Peng nevertheless succeeded, after several failures, in getting a second crop of rice, and on Wertheim's first visit in early September 1964, the green rice growing in the experimental fields looked good enough.

In autumn 1979, we met Mr. Peng again, ageing a bit but still full of energy and ideas. Liangjiafan, which in 1964 was under the jurisdiction of Baiguo subdistrict, had now been transformed into a subcommune, and Baiguo had acquired the status of a people's commune. The reason for this change seemed to be that subdistricts were typical of this region but a deviation from the general administrative order; the central authorities had decided to do away with this anomaly.[1] However, they had thus created a new departure from the usual organization at the local level: a subcommune placed as an economic and administrative unit between

---

[1] In the course of our mission we discovered that subdistricts had not been specific to Hubei province: in Sichuan province we also came across subdistricts that were *still* in existence.

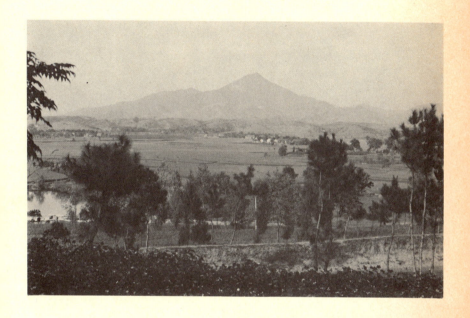

Ricefields in Liangjiafan subcommune where careful experiments by the peasants in the sixties and seventies (during the Cultural Revolution) have allowed the passage from a single rice crop to three crops per year.

*Terracing of hill slopes and regular irrigation, here
with traditional implements, have allowed to increase
productivity even on hills and traditionally poor land.
(Brigade No.3, Liangjiafan subcommune, Hubei)*

the people's commune and the brigades.[1]

Mr. Peng was at the time of our visit vice-chairman of the Revolutionary Committee of Baiguo commune, but still full of interest for developments in Liangjiafan in particular, where he even supervised some experimental fields.

The experiments to introduce a second rice crop had been successful, and the system is now applied generally in Macheng district. Peasants and cadres from other communes had come to Liangjiafan to learn from its successes.

With a certain pride Mr. Peng told us that in the course of the seventies they had even succeeded in reaping a third crop, of wheat or rapeseed, during winter.[2] This innovation had required very precise calculations of ripening periods, scientific methods (such as a selection of seeds resistant to cold) in accordance with these calculations, the right kind of manure, and plastic covers for the seedbeds of the early rice crop in order to be able to start cultivation earlier in the spring season. Modern agricultural implements to shorten the interval between the spring harvest and replanting of the late crop of rice were also important. These successes have all been obtained during the pretended "ten lost years". In other communes we visited we were also able to observe that, when one interviews peasants, one gets a much more balanced picture than the one propagated by official sources and by cadres at the provincial level, who do not stop complaining about the fatal influence of "the Gang of Four".

---

[1] The people's commune is the highest of a three-tiered system of collective rural ownership. The commune is divided into brigades that are made up of production teams. Brigades and teams are basically village or hamlet-level collectives.

[2] On his experimental fields with three crops (two rice and one wheat), 1978 total cereal yields were as high as 2,700 *jin/mou* (20 tons per hectare).

In Liangjiafan, there were certainly difficulties during the Cultural Revolution. During the first years after 1966, Mr. Peng was attacked by young commune members because "he cared more for production than for politics". But finally people had supported him, realizing that it would be too absurd to reproach a commune cadre that he cared for production.

Of a more lasting nature were certain economic difficulties that cropped up in the seventies. Liangjiafan had experienced a surplus of manpower, mainly owing to population growth and partial mechanization of agriculture. Consequently, particularly during 1968/69 and from 1972 to 1974 there was an illegal exodus towards the towns, mainly to Wuhan, by commune members in search of work.[1] In some years 300-400 people left Liangjiafan, generally taking their grain rations with them for sale on the black market. Leaders of the subcommune, however, are on the way to solving this problem.

A solution is now possible since during the seventies Liangjiafan has been able to reach self-sufficiency in cereals, even create a surplus, by increasing the number of crops. Income derived from selling the surplus to the state has strengthened the economic condition of the subcommune to such an extent that at present it has enough capital to make investments in sideline production (cotton, for example) and in livestock raising. It also succeeded, in the seventies, in developing local industries that earn a considerable income. In 1978 income from industry amounted to almost one third of total income and 20 percent of the workforce of Liangjiafan was employed in industry. Women form a considerable part of this new workforce. This increased income also helps make it possible to grant special aid to brigades and work teams in the hills, where grain production is

---

[1] Cf. E.B. Vermeer, "Social Welfare Provisions and the Limits of Inequality in Contemporary China", *Asian Survey*, Vol.19, No.9, 1979, p.858, note 2 (on Hubei province). See also E.B. Vermeer, "Patterns of Agricultural Development in Contemporary China", in Jürgen Domes (Ed.), *Chinese Politics after Mao*, 1979, p.139.

Cotton-picking on Liangjiafan subcommune, Hubei

Income derived from surplus cereal production achieved in the sixties and early seventies allowed new investments in sideline production (such as cotton) and in developing local industry.

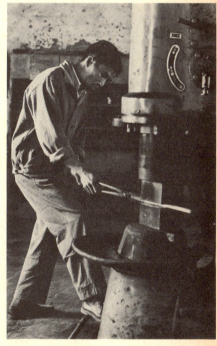

Local industry in Baiguo commune, Hubei

lower than in the plains.   (However, some of the hills have been
levelled.)   Investments in these poorer areas have become
possible because of the improved overall economic condition.

In addition, the economic strength of the subcommune was
recently further increased by the government's policy of raising
the price of grain sold to the state, on the basis of quotas
established in advance or for quantities voluntarily sold from the
surplus.

It is possible to conclude that the former strategy of
making cereals the main link in rural policy provided the means to
accomplish a transition towards the second phase of economic
development in a logical and gradual manner.   Maybe the fact that
the direction of Liangjiafan has remained in the hands of local
peasants has strengthened the bonds between cadres and peasant
masses.   Now that conditions not only for a diversification of
rural production but also for an accelerated mechanization of
agriculture have been created, the surplus of available manpower
gradually disappears.   Since 1976 those who had illegally left for
the towns have been called back as work has become available, for
example in the new industries; and quite a few of them did in fact
return.

(2) Longchi

The other people's commune presenting some interesting insights to the population question is *Longchi*, in *Emei district*, a
mountainous area in Sichuan province.   The choice of this area,
which neither of us had visited before, was a result of our
specific wish to study a region where rice was grown on terraces
on the mountain slopes, with its specific problems of isolation
and difficult access by motorized transport.   The study of such a
commune seemed important as vast areas of China are in fact
covered by mountains, presenting great production and communication problems.

The commune is situated over 200 km. to the southwest of the provincial capital of Chengdu, on the slopes of Emei mountains. In addition to rice grown on wet terraces, other crops such as maize and sweet potatoes are cultivated on slopes that are too steep for rice cultivation. Agricultural mechanization is still practically non-existent, which is understandable considering the inaccessible mountainous terrain with perpetual rains and fog; drainage is quite a problem and there is little use for tractors and other implements. There is also a relative shortage of draught animals such as mules and, consequently, the people - among them even old men and women - are forced to climb or descend the steep slopes with heavy loads on their backs. One meets many people of small stature who do not look very healthy, maybe due to shortage of iodine in the water, but also to the humid climate affecting the respiratory organs.

Population policy is one area where "modernization" has been pushed most and is most apparent. During the seventies the birth rate in Longchi commune remained rather high, as it did in other districts far from any urban centres. But during the past few years the rather youngish commune leaders, being faithful followers of Deng Xiaoping, who himself hails from Sichuan province, have introduced draconian measures of birth control, more or less patterned on the Shanghai model. For example, for their first child a couple receives a private plot even larger than the usual size allotted to commune members. For this child, free education and free medical care are provided until the age of 14. However, if a second child is born, not only are all these benefits withdrawn but the couple even has to repay all it has received for the first child.

According to birth figures provided by commune and brigade leaders, the immediate success of the measures has been tremendous. The birth rate calculated for 1978 appeared incredibly low: about eight per thousand, close to the rate in Shanghai. But we can hardly accept that such very recent measures could have had such a direct effect as early as 1978; the only real possibility is that abortion was practised on a large scale (a possibility we did not

In the mountainous area of Sichuan irrigated rice cultivation is only possible on the narrow valley bottom and some wet terraces. Other crops, such as maize or sweet potato, are cultivated on steeper, more inaccessible slopes where agricultural mechanization is practically non-existent.

(Longchi commune, Sichuan)

investigate further).   According to the district chief who
accompanied us, since 1977 the policy was to limit births per
couple to *two* children; only since the beginning of 1979 did *one*
child per couple become the accepted norm.

It was clear that the young leaders of Longchi commune and
of the subdistrict to which it belonged, who appeared not to be
local peasants but recently-appointed cadres hailing from other
places, had not considered the long-term implications of their
policy.   There are at present many children who were born during
the seventies and, consequently, for the time being there is still
plenty of manpower.   But, if each couple continues to have one
child, within some 35 years there will be a serious shortage of
young workers.   This might make life very difficult for those who
are at present young adults, but will then be old.   Since large-
scale agricultural mechanization will probably remain impossible
in this area for a long time to come, one is inclined to ask who
will perform the arduous agricultural labour.

Apparently the leaders had not sufficiently considered how
the application of general principles and directives had to be
adjusted to local circumstances requiring a specific approach.   In
this peripheral region, a "modernization" of a more traditional
and moderate type seemed much more appropriate than an automatic
copying of birth limitation methods developed elsewhere.   Large-
scale mechanization of agriculture being, for the moment, out of
the question in view of the difficulty of motorized transport, it
seems logical to give priority to the purchase and raising of
draught animals.   "Walking on four legs" would not only improve
communications with distant and isolated units of the commune up
in the mountains, it would also be a great help for old people who
are forced to carry heavy loads on their backs.

We have tried to argue with the leaders that draconian
measures, based on material incentives and negative sanctions, are
in the long run less effective than sustained efforts of mass
education and propaganda.   Fortunately, we had the impression
that though in Sichuan province in general great stress is laid on

Draconian birth control measures have been taken in Longchi commune despite the topographic limitations to agricultural mechanization and the remaining need for highly labour-intensive production techniques.

the birth control campaign, its application in Longchi commune was more rigid than in neighbouring communes or subdistricts. We also found out that the older cadres from Sichuan province and from Emei district, who accompanied us, had some doubts about the rigidity with which the new strategy was applied in Longchi.

In the economic field, certain innovations had occurred in Longchi during the Cultural Revolution. The most important new element was that since 1970 a coal mine had been exploited by the commune. The mine as such was still very primitive, but the income the commune derived from it was quite significant. Further, some new crops are now being grown on the slopes, such as medicinal herbs, tea and fruit trees, which all promise a substantial additional income. All these initiatives had been taken since 1969/1971. Some small industry has also been introduced: for example, a flour mill formerly driven by water-power (easily available but requiring a lot of manpower) was now driven by electricity. This reduced the number of workers employed in the mill but did not result in higher wages. One worker we met who had been appointed by his team to work in the mill complained that the number of work points he earned was less than when he practised agriculture.

Larger industries and more advanced mining enterprises in this region, as elsewhere, were in the hands of the state (either at the district, or at the prefecture level).

As elsewhere, we found that population size was not in itself the main problem but the relationship between manpower and employment and the strategy in this regard pursued at both central and local levels.

We were able to draw the following conclusions concerning the population issue:

The transition from the first development phase (stress laid on output per land unit) toward the second phase (stress laid on *per capita* productivity still presents exceedingly grave problems.

Brigade workers preparing a mountain slope for planting tea trees. Rapid increase in income in mountainous Longchi commune has only been possible due to diversification of production (tea and fruit plantations, medicinal herbs) and the development of coal mining.

40

Though it is reassuring that Professor Ma Yinchu has been rehabilitated and that the existence of a population problem is
officially recognized, this does not imply that the right solution
has now been found.

Whereas at first it was assumed that adoption of modern
foreign technology would be able to solve the problem of large-
scale industrial development and mechanization of agriculture
within a comparatively short time, now the leaders seem to consider that the pace of mechanization, both in agriculture and in
industry, has to be slowed down appreciably in view of the
menacing labour surplus.   Nevertheless, one still gets the
impression that the Chinese leaders wish to recover what they consider to have been "ten lost years".   As a consequence, there is
a tendency to precipitate action.   Particularly in the field of
birth control, over-hasty application of birth limitation measures
could easily upset large numbers of people whose feelings are
closely related to Chinese rural traditions.   A rapid introduction
of automation could also produce an effect opposite to what is
intended - in addition to the dangers of over-dependence on
foreign experts and foreign capital.

But it is in particular in the rural areas that undue haste
may prove self-defeating.   Great Leaps Forward are as dangerous
in the eighties as they were in the fifties.

If the Chinese were prepared to acknowledge the remarkable
successes achieved in the course of the three earlier decades, it
would become much easier to initiate the second development phase
as an accelerated continuation of strategies already followed in
the past.

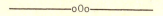

PART II

EQUALITY AND INEQUALITY

A. <u>Historical Outline</u>

In pre-revolutionary China inequality was characteristic of rural society.   Two social layers, gentry and peasantry, were clearly distinguishable.   Though there were some chances for individuals from the peasantry to penetrate into the gentry by cultural achievement, for example if patronage provided them with the education required to pass the state examinations, such cases remained rare.

The revolution that in 1949 led to establishment of the People's Republic of China embodied the idea of the fundamental equality of all citizens.   All traditional privileges were to be swept away.   Perhaps no revolution in human history has gone such a long way in its attempts to take the concept of equality seriously.

As far as rural society is concerned, it is mainly the economic aspects of the equality vs. inequality issue that are of interest to us.   Inequalities based on social status also played a significant role in traditional rural societies, the gentry enjoying a prestige far superior to the mass of the peasantry and being able to exploit it in all kinds of relationships with individual peasant families.   But in post-revolutionary China the specific prerogatives of the gentry were radically discarded. Therefore, it is mainly the remaining economic inequalities, which in themselves are significant enough, which concern us here.

Marxism as an ideology is certainly not egalitarian, and this also applies to its Maoist version.   At most one could call the terminal station - the ultimate arrival at the true "communist society" - egalitarian, because of the principle: to each according to his needs. But Marxist theory has always assumed that this terminal phase could be attained only under conditions of plenty - that is to say at the "Greek calends". While scarcity prevails, a socialist society, characterized by the principle "from each according to his capacity, to each according to his labour", is the best one attainable. This also corresponds with the Maoist idea that the system of remuneration should help to stimulate production.

Far from being egalitarian, this concept of a "socialist society" is thus characterized by remuneration according to achievement - the same principle which also according to a capitalist point of view *should* be decisive for economic behaviour. Whereas, however, under a capitalist system private ownership of means of production (land and capital) can also be a source of individual income, this ownership in a socialist society is in principle either nationalized and thus transformed into state ownership, or turned into collective ownership.

For rural society in China collective ownership and management are of far greater importance than state ownership. Workers in state farms get fixed salaries, which are more or less equalized all over the country, but remuneration is differentiated according to the type of work performed. In a state farm for returned "Overseas" Chinese in Guangdong province, visited by Wertheim, the salaries are graded according to categories. Newcomers get 24 *yuan* per month; first category 32; second category 37; third 41.5; fourth 48 *yuan*. The average salary is 38 *yuan*. It seems, however, that salaries higher than the official maximum are possible: an experienced driver, already a grandfather, stated that he earned over 60 *yuan* a month. Income differentials are, therefore, related to the division of salaried workers into different categories, just as they are in state industries.

But the main source of economic inequality in the countryside is to be found in collective agriculture. From the middle fifties onwards Chinese agriculture has been collectivized, except

for small private plots mainly used for growing vegetables or
fodder. Within each collective unit, remuneration depends in
principle upon the quantity and quality of work performed, calculated according to the number of earned work points per day. As
far as individual reward is concerned, the performed work is
decisive. There is also a growing tendency for women to receive
an equal amount of work points as men for equal work whereas in
the sixties it was still usual for women to earn on average about
seven or eight work points for a full day's work, compared with a
man's nine or ten work points. What was considered as typically
women's work, for example cotton or tea picking, was generally
valued with less points than "typical male work". But in the early
seventies, at the time of the campaign "to criticize Confucius",
which was at the same time directed against all forms of discrimination against women, a campaign in which the so-called Gang of
Four led by Jiang Qing was most active[1], started aiming at a more
consistent application of the equal-pay-for-equal-work principle
in the rural sphere. For example, the newspapers carried articles
urging rural women to convince their menfolk how heavy and back-
breaking typically "female" work could be. Nevertheless, sexual
inequalities in remuneration are not yet a thing of the past.

Of course, the welfare level of a family is not only dependent on the physical strength and technical qualifications of
individual workers, but also on the number of full-time or half-
time workers per family. This, of course, has an effect on family
planning. On the one hand, few children, or a planned spacing of
births, may enable a married woman to work full-time, and thus to
increase the family income appreciably. On the other hand, in a

---

[1] An excellent article by the French sinologist Michelle Loi, who
visited China both in 1974 and in 1976, examines the position
of women: "Les femmes chinoises et la 'Quatrième corde", in
Questions féministes, No.6 (September 1979), pp.35 ff. The
author observes that the campaign had enormous support in 1974
from the female masses, but that the cadres, including those
who were leading the Women's Federation, were most reserved in
accepting these new ideas.

Woman worker in commune industry, Dali, Guangdong

In spite of a campaign, launched in the early seventies, to stop sexual discrimination, to open "typical male jobs" to women and to apply consistently the equal-pay-equal-work principle, sexual inequalities in remuneration remain important, and "easy" work, such as cotton sorting that earns few work points, remains often typical women's work.

Cotton sorting in Liangjiafan subcommune, Hubei

long-term perspective a family may see it as in its interest to have more children to contribute to the family income. This may cause a clash between perceived family interests and collective interests as perceived by the leadership.

The prevalent system implies that *within* a collective unit, that functions as a "unit of account", there exists uniformity as to the value of a work point. But what is to be distributed depends on total production, and consequently on the total income of the unit concerned.

When in 1958 the people's communes were created, it was assumed that the commune, which usually consisted of tens of thousands of members plus their dependents, could function as a "unit of account". In practice this meant that the value of each work point, calculated on the basis of the total income of the commune, could be uniform for all its members. Therefore, within the commune, inequality would exist only in so far as performance, and thus the number of work points earned, were unequal.

But there could be considerable differences *among* people's communes according to their total income, which also implies commensurate differences in the value of a work point which varies directly with the rise or fall of collective profits. For example, communes in the neighbourhood of big cities, which could profit from the availability of nightsoil from the city, as well as from an urban consuming market for vegetables, fruit, meat, fowl and eggs, were generally more prosperous than communes situated deeper inland. Similarly, in plains and valleys yields were generally much higher than in hilly or mountainous regions.

But even with this limitation of the socialist principle of equal reward for equal work to the radius of a people's commune as a collective unit, its application proved, for the time being, beyond the reach of Chinese rural society. Each people's commune was, and is, divided into brigades, and these again into production teams. Within the confines of one commune the geographic situation may vary considerably and consequently the level of welfare among brigades and teams may also show great variations. Soon after 1958 the Chinese leaders realized that equalizing the value of a work point for all members - and consequently for all production teams - within a people's commune seriously affected the incentive to maximum effort. Those members of a team with infertile land up in the hills might have reasoned as follows: why should we work as hard as possible if in the end we will share in the wealth earned on behalf of the whole commune with appreciably less effort by teams in the river valleys from their fertile clay soil? On the other hand, members of teams in favoured locations were little inclined to make great efforts either. Why, they could argue, should we drudge if the results of our work will be spread evenly over the entire commune?[1]

Such reactions showed that the sense of collective solidarity generally did not yet transcend the level of the production team, where people knew one another well and could keep an eye upon each other. The Chinese leadership drew its conclusions from such experiences and reduced the size of the unit of account, within which the value of a work point was equalized, at first to the brigade level and then, when even this proved too ambitious, to the production team level. This happened in 1963 - and in 1975 it was even written into the Constitution that for the time being, as a general rule, the production team had to function as the basic accounting unit.[2] This provision in the Constitution was intended as a counter-measure against a tendency that had arisen in the course of the Cultural Revolution to again raise the unit of account to the brigade level, as an element of a policy aiming in the long run at a greater egalitarianism. Present regulations allow the raising of the unit to the brigade level only if certain conditions are fulfilled.

---

[1] See, for example, Isabel and David Cook, *The First Years of Yangyi Commune*, London, 1966, p.38.

[2] In the Constitution of 1978 (article 7) this principle is confirmed.

According to the Maoist concept, in the future the level of the units of account and of collective ownership should be gradually raised to the brigade, and finally to the commune level. A last step would be for collective ownership to give way to state ownership, which would imply that the people's communes are all transformed into state farms, which pay fixed salaries not keyed to unit output.   But even this last phase - which, again, sounds like what should happen at the "Greek calends"[1] - would not do away with inequality; it would merely eliminate variations in local conditions of production, but for the rest it would keep the socialist system of remuneration - to each according to his labour - intact.

Therefore, we may conclude that the remuneration system in China is far from egalitarian; nor does it aim at egalitarianism. There is even an inbuilt element in the rural economic system that may be seen as an embodiment of an anti-egalitarian principle: the prevalent tax system.

Since the late fifties the tax paid by collective units has been established as a fixed amount in accordance with factors such as soil fertility, as assessed at that time. If production rises, the total amount of tax due in principle remains equal, which means that as a percentage of earned income the tax goes down. In fact, this system strongly favours those people's communes in the neighbourhood of cities that already enjoy a comparatively high level of prosperity. The declining percentage of income to be set aside for taxes (which around 1970 in communes near great cities had often dropped to some 1.5 or 2 percent, from about 14 percent in the late fifties), also enables these collective units to earmark an ever larger proportion of their income for new investments. *De facto*, therefore, the tax system in China is neither proportional nor progressive - but usually the opposite. The poor units have to pay a *greater* proportion of their income as taxes than the

---

[1] René Dumont, *Chine, La révolution culturale*, Paris, 1976, warns against actually implementing this official goal (p.188).

richer ones. This may be a good spur to production but is definitely without trace of egalitarianism. However, provincial or county authorities sometimes exonerate poor units from taxes for a time as a form of subsidy.

On the other hand, from the sixties onwards there has been a serious effort to guarantee a minimum subsistence level to each inhabitant. Even since the fifties the principle was officially proclaimed that each household should enjoy "the five guarantees", namely: food, clothing, fuel, education of children and burial. This principle has been constantly upheld during the past three decades, although its application has been strongly influenced by the decentralized character of rural administration. To quote Vermeer: "Provision of social welfare is, in the first place, a duty of small groups (family, village, factory), and only after that fails does the State take over".[1] Children are not only by custom but also legally obliged to take care of their parents if they are no longer able to work (although collective units try to find light work for old people as long as possible). This implies that social welfare is required only for the few cases when the relatives cannot support disabled persons such as elderly people, the handicapped, widows and orphans. Each collective unit has to set aside a small percentage (some two percent) of its income as a collective welfare fund, although the amount of aid paid out to a family is not uniform but determined in each case by the leader-ship of the unit. In some richer brigades or communes, mainly in the vicinity of large towns, pensions (often in kind) have been introduced for the old.

In practice, at least as important as direct aid is the custom that in each unit the greatest part of the collectively-produced grain is distributed in kind as "basic grain", which gua-rantees a minimum consumption level. The remainder is distributed

---

[1] Eduard B. Vermeer, "Social Welfare Provisions and the Limits of Inequality in Contemporary China", *Asian Survey*, Vol.19, No.9, 1979, p.879.

as work point grain"; the work points earned by each worker are calculated on the basis of the work point value as a percentage of total collective income. This means that there may be "people who have received more advances of grain than their due according to the year-end account"; in that case, unless it is decided that they will receive assistance from the production team's or brigade's welfare fund, which rarely happens, they will become indebted to the team. But according to Vermeer "mass-scale indebtment has an egalitarian effect if repayment cannot or can only be partly enforced, which is obviously the case in many instances".[1]

It is understandable therefore, that the people's commune was considered by the peasants as "an iron rice-bowl that nobody can break".

However, there were people's communes or smaller collective units that had to face serious difficulties, either permanently or temporarily (e.g. in the case of natural calamities). During the sixties it was general policy to provide state assistance to the relatively less-developed regions of the country. This could be realized, for example, "by identifying really poor production units, scientifically determining the reasons for their poverty, and trying to solve their peculiar problems by giving them massive financial and technical assistance".[2]

In 1963 state assistance was systematized with the creation of the Agricultural Bank of China. A great deal of assistance was provided in the form of loans. The Agricultural Bank also had trained agricultural scientists, hydrologists etc. on its staff, in order to examine the technical aspects of loan applications and

---

[1] Idem, pp. 871/72.

[2] Shahid J. Burki, *A Study of Chinese Communes - 1965*, Cambridge (Mass.), 1969, p. 31.

to propose important changes in the project blueprints submitted
by the communes.   This system of state assistance to poor regions
also could serve to reduce economic disparity between rural
regions, for example between those on the plains and those in the
mountains.

As a general assessment of the situation in Chinese rural
society before the Cultural Revolution of 1966/1967 we may conclude that inequalities were present not so much among different
social groups as among different economic units, and that the most
important source of inequality was divergence in geographic,
climatic and soil conditions, which accounted for highly variable
incomes of collective units used as a basis for calculating the
value of a work point.   These differences were somewhat mitigated
by specific provisions for assisting poor units financially and
technologically.

Within each collective unit the "socialist" principle of
remuneration still operated in so far as appreciable differences
existed in the *number* of work points earned by each individual,
although the *value* of a work point was equalized within the
collectivity functioning as the accounting unit (mostly, since
1963, the production team).   However, the number of active workers
within a family of course played an important role; in this way
the creation of people's communes functioned indirectly as a significant stimulus to family planning, because a smaller number or
a diligent spacing of children could release married women from
being overburdened by household drudgery.   On the other hand, distribution of "basic grain", and social relief in exceptional cases,
to a certain extent alleviated the inequalities inherent in the
"socialist" remuneration system.

The Cultural Revolution, started in 1966, in some respects
brought about substantial changes in rural policies, as far as the
equality-inequality issue is concerned.   The most important change
was adopting Dazhai brigade in an unfertile hilly area as a model
for commune management.   Two aspects of holding up Dazhai as a
model should be stressed.

First of all, presenting Dazhai as a model from which those engaged in agriculture should learn, expressed the new principle that henceforth people's communes and the smaller collective units should "rely on their own forces".[1] Dazhai brigade had succeeded in attaining a comparatively high level of production, in spite of an extremely unfavourable location, by demonstrating great inventiveness and by a huge collective effort. The conclusion drawn from this example and other similar success stories was that backwardness was not due to unfavourable conditions but to lack of political consciousness and of revolutionary fervour. When Wertheim revisited China during the winter of 1970/1971, he found that backward brigades or production teams were no longer considered as units in need of financial support. Allegedly what was needed was political support from the commune, for example by lending good cadres to the weaker units and thereby improving the quality of its leadership. The underlying philosophy was that any collective unit had to assess its own potential resources and to find out how to develop them so as to extract a maximum yield.

Of course, there was a great danger that, in spite of the underlying philosophy that strong and weak units should equally exploit their potential for growth, the principle that each unit should rely on its own forces would, in actual practice, strongly favour those units that started with an initial advantage. The consequence would be that existing divergences in level of welfare between different regions or people's communes would widen instead of narrowing.[2] However, there were also aspects that mitigated

---

[1] Today the Chinese leadership alleges that Dazhai has in fact received a lot of external assistance to make it a model case.

[2] W.F. Wertheim pointed out this danger in "Polarity and Equality in the Chinese People's Communes", *Revue des Pays de l'Est*, Vol. 15, 1974, pp.17/18; from the same author: "Rainbow Bridge Revisited", 2nd part, *Eastern Horizon*, Vol.11, 1972, No.1, p.37. See also recently Ng Gek-boo, "The Commune System and Income Inequality in Rural China", *Bulletin of Concerned Asian Scholars*, Vol.11, No.3, 1979; and Keith Griffin and Ashwani Saith, *The Pattern of Income Inequality in Rural China*, Working Paper ILO, 1980.

existing inequalities, particularly those *within* a given commune. Wertheim observed that in certain communes if, for example, one brigade, owing to a less favourable location in the hills, possessed rather infertile sandy soils, a neighbouring brigade provided clay from a river valley to mix with the sand. Whereas in earlier times the poorer brigade or team would have had to pay for anything it received from another brigade or team, either in goods or in services, in the early seventies a free exchange between units was considered to be a matter of mutual solidarity.

In another study, based on research in August 1971, it was found that also at that time several devices were used to "remove polarity" in rural areas.[1] In certain cases the state still provided special interest-free credits to less advanced communes in order to help them increase their capital investments. *Within* the commune it was an accepted practice that commune cadres were sent to the less advanced brigades to help them ideologically and technically. Though backwardness was not considered to be "a matter of money" a commune could finance industries and defray "major expenses for such items as water-pumps and schools which were beyond the means of individual brigades or production teams."

Further, ideological training was provided by announcing "all progress made by teams or brigades" on the loudspeaker system owned by the commune. They were also publicized on large wall posters displayed at several places in the commune. Another device used by a propaganda department of a people's commune was to give training to so-called "barefoot correspondents" able to present achievements in an "original and artistic way" on wall posters, to "cultural workers who can sing and dance and give performances to put across ideological lessons", and to "story-tellers who can declaim revolutionary historic events in a vivid and fascinating manner".

---

[1] L. Ch. Schenk-Sandbergen, "How the Chinese People remove Polarity within their Countryside", *Eastern Horizon*, Vol.12, No.3, 1973, pp.8 ff.

Experts from advanced research institutes were also still being sent to weaker communes.

Therefore, although financial assistance to weak units was appreciably reduced during the Cultural Revolution, this does not imply that these units were at that time left to sink or swim.

Another aspect of "learning from Dazhai" was a certain change in the way of allocating and calculating work points. Following his visit in 1970/1971 Wertheim wrote:[1]

> "There were reports about a radical change in the remuneration system; material incentives were said to have been relinquished in favour of moral incentives. My main impression has been that the changes were less fundamental than would appear from such reports... The system of remuneration is still described as a socialist one: 'to each according to his work'. The terminology has become more radical: material incentives are now frowned upon. One now often hears people say that one should not work for the sake of acquiring as many work points as possible, but in order to further the common good. But all the same, work points still do exist and create differential incomes among people belonging to the same collective. There is a certain change in the criteria applied for the calculation of one's merits: a correct political and ideological attitude demonstrated through a thorough application to study Mao Zedong's thought, a correct working style and a devotion to the common cause, is now mentioned as the first criterion used in assessing one's merit, as a basis for establishing the number of work points earned. However, physical strength and special qualifications also figure among the criteria mentioned. Upon my question in one commune in Zhejiang province, whether a worker with a correct attitude would get the same rating irrespective of physical strength or qualifications the reply was definitely: no! If the morale of two workers is equally high, they said, it is still achievement that counts: 'to each according to his work'!"

However, it is not certain to what extent this reply could be generalized.

---

[1] W.F. Wertheim, "Polarity and Equality in the Chinese People's Commune", *op.cit.*, pp.13/14.

"Learning from Dazhai", as far as the system of assessing work points is concerned, had more to do with a change in the *period* for which one's work points were calculated (periods of three months, half a year or even a full year instead of a very cumbersome daily registration) than with a change in the principle of differentiating between individuals according to their achievement as workers in a collective unit. However, during the seventies a greater stress was laid on equal pay for equal work regardless of sex.

B. Recent Developments and Present Trends

Our general impression during our exploratory mission was that official views regarding the inequality issue have appreciably shifted. The "socialist" principle ("to each according to his labour") is being stressed much more strongly than in the early seventies, when, in determining work points, account was also taken of one's level of ideological motivation. At present, it has become the vogue, both in industry and in agriculture, to stimulate workers to greater achievements by *material* incentives. Whereas during the Cultural Revolution bonuses were largely rejected (sometimes as "sugar-coated bullets"), at present they are again playing a significant role.[1] In many enterprises, also in the countryside, a system has been introduced that is not unlike piece-work wages. Whoever over-fulfils a norm established for a certain type of work receives a bonus; this not only applies to individuals but also to enterprises or collective units, such as production teams. If the norm has not been fulfilled, one gets less than full pay. Again, this applies equally to individuals and collective units.

---

[1] Even during the Cultural Revolution bonuses were introduced in certain areas. We found, for example, that in the coal mines of Longchi commune (Emei district) the bonus system was introduced in 1969 and has been maintained since.

In principle, this new system threatens to result in increasing inequality. From official pronouncements one gets the impression that this inequality is no longer viewed as an evil, or even as a temporary but inevitable one, as was the case during the Cultural Revolution. The present leadership accepts this inequality as a matter of principle, provided that it stimulates production and "modernization". In the course of 1979 the Chinese press published articles in which collective units and individuals were both urged to "enrich themselves". It was argued, following the pattern of thinking prevalent in Third World countries known as "betting on the strong"[1], that in this way the richer production teams would "serve as models which could stimulate the poorer ones to follow their example". *Beijing Review*[2] went still further, arguing that "enriching oneself first" was actually an egalitarian principle because, in the long run, it would lead to less inequality since poorer units or individuals would increasingly compete with the richer ones!

Evidently, the "Negative Lessons from the Third World"[3] have not yet been fully digested in China. These lessons teach that "betting on the strong", propagated as a means of inducing the weaker ones to follow the model set by the strong ones, quite often has the opposite effect. Following the example of the strong presupposes the possession of sufficient cultivable land, irrigation water and capital. Mostly it is exactly these factors that are lacking among the weaker sections of the peasantry. Consequently, the richer farmers do not pull their poorer colleagues

---

[1] Cf. W.F. Wertheim, "Betting on the Strong", Chapter 12 of *East-West Parallels: Sociological Approaches to Modern Asia*, The Hague, 1964; from the same author: "Aid to the Poor - Or Betting on the Poor?", in *Development of Societies: The Next Twenty-Five Years*, proceedings of the ISS 25th Anniversary Conference, December 1977, The Hague, 1979, pp.86 ff.

[2] *Beijing Review*, 2 March 1979.

[3] Title of lecture delivered by Wertheim in Beijing on 18 October 1979.

along on their way towards progress, but grow richer at the
expense of the "weak".

It seems that in the past income ceilings were fixed by pre-
fectures and districts, but by 1977 they appear to have been
abolished.   It was stated in recent Chinese pronouncements that
"it is sheer illusion to suppose socialism can be built by
deliberately preventing people from getting rich", and that "it is
equally absurd to maintain a low-income level for people in relatively prosperous areas or units to prevent a possible polarization of society".[1] Some of the Shanghai radicals ("Gang of Four")
were more conscious of the danger of growing polarization, as a
consequence of the mechanization of agriculture. They were afraid
that a technological revolution would lead to a widening of the
gap between different regions and collective units.[2]

To a greater extent than during the early seventies, individuals are also allowed to enrich themselves, though still within
certain bounds of a collective rural economy, by exploiting
private plots and by selling their produce on free markets.   The
potential for inequalities between individuals to multiply is thus
also increased.   The recently introduced responsibility system in
agriculture that, in some cases, confers responsibility for production on individual households is also likely to further increase inequalities at the local level.

As well as offering material incentives to stimulate production, the present leadership shows a certain tendency to favour
investment in advanced areas, where "stable and high yields" can
be obtained.   As long ago as 1975, in his speech at "Dazhai
conference", Hua Guofeng drew specific attention to so-called key
districts of the Dazhai type, where agricultural mechanization had

---

[1] E.B. Vermeer, op.cit., p.874, with references to New China News
Agency, 19 February 1979.

[2] See for example Yao Wenyuan in *The Red Flag* of March 1975.

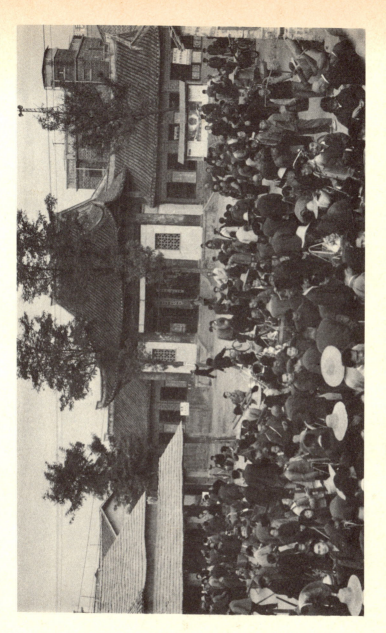

The extension of free markets, where individuals or collectivities can sell the produce of their private plots or surplus above quota provides an important source of extra income but increases greatly the potential for increased rural inequalities. (Early morning 'free market' in Macheng, Hubei.)

made considerable headway. During the past few years, the stress on state investments in the "large commercial bases" of grain and cotton appears to have been increased and, according to Vermeer, such "priorities will increase differences in development levels."[1]

Another aspect of the present "modernization" drive that may well lead to increasing inequalities between rich and poor units is the policy of stressing specialization of production according to local comparative advantages. This policy is most likely to hit the poor regions, particularly those with difficulties of communications and transport, unless they were to receive compensation via redistributive fiscal policies - at present unlikely.

The present Chinese leaders are accusing the "Gang of Four" of obstructing and sabotaging production by their "egalitarian" policies in the earlier seventies, the consequences of which had been "that everyone remained poor". In the press and in talks with provincial cadres the impression is quite often given that the "socialist" principle of "to each according to his labour" was fully relinquished during the Cultural Revolution. As we have already observed, reality was less clear-cut than this.

In the Chinese press of late 1979 and early 1980 there was a discussion on the tenability of the principle of the unbreakable iron rice bowl. Certain authors argued that it functions merely as a stimulus to laziness and laxity, and as an irresponsible form of relying on the collectivity. This public debate shows that even the guarantee of a minimal satisfaction of basic needs, one of the greatest achievements of the People's Republic of China, is being questioned, in a sequel to the present "enrich yourself" policies.

---

[1] E.B. Vermeer, *op.cit.*, p.874, referring to a speech by Hua Guofeng in March 1978. For an interesting analysis of the impact that the new rural policies will have on the inequality issue; see also Peter Nolan and Gordon White, "Distribution and Development in China", *Bulletin of Concerned Asian Scholars*, Vol.13, No.3, 1981, pp.2 ff.   In many respects, and even in several details, Nolan's and White's analysis is in accordance with our findings during our mission in China.

C. Experiences during UNRISD Mission

It struck us during our mission that though there is an outspoken policy to keep the work team as a unit of account, except for exceptional cases[1], during our tour of the Chinese countryside we were repeatedly confronted with local deviations from this policy.   In a people's commune near Beijing visited by Wertheim, four out of ten brigades were units of account, as were 10 out of 13 in a tea commune near Hangzhou (the famous *Xihu* commune).   The explanation of the difference given here was that in tea-growing brigades the workers are living in closely-built houses, and great differentials in income between households are absent.On the other hand, in those few brigades of Xihu where grain is the main crop, habitation is more dispersed, which accounts for a greater economic role of the smaller units, viz. production teams.In other communes visited by Wertheim during the first part of the mission it was still the production team that was the unit of account.

One could therefore suppose that brigades as units of account were mainly to be found in more advanced areas.

(1) Tuyuan

It was a surprise, therefore, for us to find that in Tuyuan commune, Xinhui district of Guangdong province, which by no means had the appearance of a prosperous community, there were also brigades that had been recently raised to units of account.   This made it possible for us to study the consequences of such a change in greater detail.

Tuyuan is situated some 15 kms. from the district capital of Xinhui.   Though near the Delta plains of Guangdong province, it has some characteristics in common with the hilly and mountainous areas of the western part of the province.   Topographically, the

---

[1] Article 7 of the Constitution of 1978.

area is composed of small plains, flat valleys and scattered hills that occupy about 30 percent of the area. At the bottom of the hills the slopes are terraced, and groundnuts, soya and sweet potato are grown. Where the terraces are irrigated, rice is grown as in the plains. Though Xinhui county is somewhat above the average income level of Guangdong province, Tuyuan commune is below the average of the county and can be considered as being not far from the overall average in the southern regions.

Wertheim had already visited the commune in 1964, and had noted it at that time as one much nearer to the average commune than those generally visited by tourists or delegations. Soils in this area do not seem particularly fertile, a great deal of them being lateritic; and, as it is not far from the South Chinese Sea, Tuyuan is quite often ravaged by typhoons.

The first experiment in raising the unit of account to the brigade level was undertaken in one brigade of the commune in 1969. Within this brigade the members found they could develop production much faster than if a small production team were the unit of account, and that they could raise their own individual welfare accordingly. Peasants from other brigades came to the conclusion that a production team was too weak to improve the infrastructural basis of agriculture and to develop sidelines of production. This is why at the end of 1977 six more brigades (out of a total of 20 in Tuyuan commune) applied to raise the level of the unit of account. According to the rules, this is possible, under the following four conditions:

1. It should be in accordance with the expressed wish of the members of the units concerned;
2. The application should be supported by the cadres of the brigade and teams concerned;
3. Differences in output between the production teams should not be too great;
4. The brigade should not be too dispersed geographically.

Anyway, ratification by the commune and district authorities is required.   In the case of the six brigades cited, permission was given provisionally on an experimental basis.

Those brigades that had applied for the new arrangement were actually those where the level of productivity among teams was about equal; moreover, they were mostly brigades that were not too populous (ranging from 800 to 1,400 people).   Those where the production team has remained the accounting unit are generally bigger.

We were interested in the consequences of the new arrangement for calculating the value of a work point.   It appears that since the new system has operated no production teams exist any more.   The work is distributed among groups, which are allotted specific tasks and have to fulfil norms in order to earn, as a group, a certain number of work points.   If they surpass the norm, they get more points; if they do not attain it, they get less than the agreed number of points.   The group itself distributes work points among the members.

Consequently, no absolute equality of remuneration among work groups of the brigade is aimed at. It appears that, though on average individual incomes have been somewhat raised since the innovation, for members of *some* of the former production teams (the richer ones) income may have gone down.   In order to raise it they have to work longer per day.   The brigade leaders admit that when the idea of introducing the new system was discussed among the masses, peasants belonging to richer production teams had some reservations; they were afraid of a downward levelling of incomes, which they also called "transition in poverty" (*qiong guodu*).   But they have come to the conclusion that, according to experience since the fifties, only large collective units are able to guarantee increases in productivity, particularly as far as hydraulic works are concerned.   For example, unified planning of irrigation works became possible through raising the level of the unit of account, and in this way conflicts of interest between production teams could be resolved, and the labour force be more rationally used.   The same applies to earmarking funds for investments

63

(production teams are too small for it).

For the specific brigade (*Longmian* Brigade) that we studied, it had been calculated that, according to the production plan for 1978, gross total income of the brigade would rise from 213,000 to 400,000 *yuan* after the raising of accounting unit to brigade level. In fact it reached only 372,000 *yuan*; however, the average income of the members even surpassed the average income of the richest production team in 1977. The most important innovation had been a significant extension of a bamboo workshop, which was able to increase its labour force from 27 to 70, and thus add significantly to the brigade's income. Other sidelines have been added in rather recent years, for example collective pig farming, and a brick factory.[1]/

It seems, therefore, that in spite of serious official objections to a raising of the level of units of account[2]/, even in not-too-prosperous communes there may be strong arguments for doing so. It would be interesting to know whether the innovation, which had so far been allowed only on an experimental basis, has been definitely approved by the higher authorities, or will be. The system as it stands is certainly not egalitarian. Individual differences, expressed in the number of work points earned per individual worker or household, remain fully in force. On the other hand, equalization occurs within a brigade as regards the *value* of a work point. But the system of granting extra work points to work groups who exceed the norm and deducting them from those who lag behind accounts for a new source of inequality. Moreover, bonuses for output exceeding the norm could lead to a stress on quantity to the detriment of quality of work.

---

[1]/ Appendix II shows the complete Production Plan and Projections for 1979 for Longmian Brigade. It shows more generally how a brigade economy functions, how revenues, the value of work points and distribution to brigade members are calculated.

[2]/ Vermeer, *op.cit.*, pp.858/59, mentions some of the objections officially raised or assumed by him to be of some relevance.

The raising of the unit of account to the brigade level in Longmian
Brigade had made a more rational and planned use of investment funds
possible and allowed a significant extension of a bamboo workshop.
(Longmian Brigade, Tuyuan Commune, Guangdong)

Tuyuan commune also offered other experiences relevant to the inequality issue. The way the slogans of "learning from Dazhai" and "relying on one's own forces" were implemented during the Cultural Revolution could hardly be called satisfactory. Whereas in the first half of the sixties (1960-1965) the commune, as a comparatively weak unit, had received 600,000 *yuan* from the state for infrastructural works, this support was stopped at the time of the Cultural Revolution. In 1970 the commune again received some assistance (60,000 *yuan*) but nothing from 1971 to 1976. The same was true for the whole Xinhui district. Evidently Tuyuan could not do without outside support; for example, it had experienced serious difficulties when the pinewoods, planted in the hills since Liberation, became badly infested with caterpillars at the end of the sixties. Part of the woods had to be cut down, and only in 1973 was the pest brought under control, by biological and chemical methods, so that replanting could start (no longer as a monoculture). Other problems arose because the rice crops were often affected by typhoons or heavy rainfall.

Rice production had hardly risen in Tuyuan commune since Wertheim visited it in 1964, though total population figures showed an appreciable increase. (While from 1964 to 1978 the irrigated land surface had increased by about 35 percent, population increased by about 25 percent, total cereal production increased only by about 18 percent and productivity per land unit remained more or less stagnant.)

This does not mean that for Tuyuan the Cultural Revolution and its aftermath had really been "ten lost years". During the seventies some new initiatives were taken; for example, from 1975 onwards, important improvements were made in the construction of a large reservoir which had been started during the Great Leap Forward (1958/1959). The work, with state assistance of 30,000 *yuan*, was completed in 1978.

Further, from 1975 onwards the initiative was taken to build pig sties for collective pig raising (formerly pigs had only been raised privately).

Yet it was clear that the commune had had difficulties in "relying on its own forces". Some of the commune arrangements we observed may have functioned as a drag upon economic development; for example, the electricity rate charged by the state for industrial purposes, 0.30 *yuan* per kw/hour, is exceedingly high; for agricultural purposes it is much lower (0.05 *yuan*), and even for lighting it is lower than for industry: 0.24 *yuan*. The state itself pays only 0.07 *yuan* for electricity generated from the reservoir, which belongs to the commune. This regulation, which is valid for the whole district, regardless of the wealth of the commune, might operate as a disincentive for industrial development.

From 1977 onwards, the commune was again receiving considerable sums from the state for investment (140,000 *yuan* for 1977 and 1978). It is possible that people in Guangdong province, which borders on Hong Kong and Macao, are generally relying too much on outside help, a reliance that could be stimulated by the frequency of remittances from relatives living outside China. In a recent publication based on experiences in Fujian province, which also has close relationships with Hong Kong, the adverse effects of peasant families receiving overseas remittances are clearly exposed.[1] Because of the availability of this surplus income "the able-bodied men need not work diligently on the farm", and a black market is stimulated. The collective economy functioned much better, according to the author, in villages where *no* peasants were regularly receiving remittances or gifts.

We do not suggest that Tuyuan's special difficulties result from similar causes and, in the few days we spent there, we did not investigate this possibility. It does seem likely, however, that the principle of "relying on one's own forces" could encounter more problems in Guangdong province than in other parts of China that are farther removed from the temptations and influence of the capitalist world.

---

[1] Elena S.H. Yu, "Overseas Remittances in South-eastern China", *The China Quarterly*, No.78, June 1979, pp.339 ff.

There is one final point in connection with the inequality issue in Tuyuan commune. There exists a general directive that poorer collective units should earmark at least 60 percent of their gross income for distribution among the workers, as a basis for calculating the value of a work point (part of it being paid out in kind). Richer communes may distribute less (some 50 percent), which for the time being contributes to some levelling of personal income between richer and poorer units but which, on the other hand, strongly favours the richer ones as far as a potential for further investments and capital accumulation is concerned (in the same way as the prevailing tax system favours richer collective units).[1] However, in Tuyuan commune which is definitely not a rich one, we found that in a brigade (Longmian) that had been raised to a unit of account, only 42 percent of the gross income was distributed among the workers.[2] The remaining 58 percent was earmarked for taxes and "current expenses" (which term in this case included, as well as the social fund, also about 7 percent for investments). It seems that these percentages had already been in force a long time. According to the Chairman of the commune, the more advanced brigades paid out 53 percent or 54 percent of gross income to the workers, whereas those with a comparatively low income paid out no more than 40 percent. The Chairman stated that such low percentages might be due to laxity and thriftless management. This means that the system applied was the exact reverse of the general directive urging *poor* units to pay *higher* percentages!

It is quite possible that, owing to the absence of substantial state assistance from 1966 onwards, the commune and its constituting units in this way tried at least to keep part of their income for investment, to the detriment of immediate consumption.

1/ Burki, *op.cit.*, pp.28-31.

2/ Distribution to brigade members made up 38.9% only of gross agricultural revenue and 46% of gross industrial revenue, giving an average distribution of 42.5% of total gross revenue (see Appendix II).

But the system might well have had an opposite effect: low wages are not likely to stimulate a great effort in production. A decent living standard guaranteed by collective farming could be precisely a precondition for an effective functioning of a socialist system.

Tuyuan, it is clear, offers plenty of scope for studying the contradiction between long-term interests (a high investment rate) and short-term interests (a reasonable level of living for the workers).

(2) *Liuji*

Another place where we found a stark deviation from the general policy regarding units of account is Liuji commune, Xinzhou district in Hubei province. Liuji is not very populous; in 1964, when Wertheim paid his first visit, it had over 6,000 inhabitants; at present it is combined with two other communes, and has a population of about 23,000.

The commune is situated about 70 km. northeast from Wuhan; Xinzhou district is known as a Dazhai-type county (a "key" district for agricultural mechanization). Xinzhou district, including Liuji commune, is especially advanced in cotton growing. It is a relatively prosperous commune where about 50 percent of the gross income is distributed among the workers.

The most striking feature about Liuji is that from the start in 1958 it had always been the unit of account. At present this commune consists of 12 brigades and 116 production teams (which means that, contrary to Tuyuan, these lower units have been kept intact; the only specialized team is that engaged in fishery). In 1962 Liuji got an order to lower the level of account to the brigade level; but the members had serious objections. They did not see how they could divide the machinery they had acquired since collectivization in 1957. Moreover, at that time the commune was rather small. They had their way, evidently without getting into conflict with the district and now claim that they were entitled to refuse to implement the general directive.

When Liuji was combined in 1965 with *Taijia* commune, where at that time the brigade was the unit of account, there was no opposition to raising it to the commune level. The combination resulted in all brigades being able to raise the value of work points. In 1976, the commune was combined with *Dadu* commune (which also already functioned as a unit of account), because this facilitated the construction of a good irrigation system (Dadu was upstream, Liuji downstream). Furthermore, a more rational use of the machinery could thus be ensured (Liuji had more machinery than Dadu).

Although here the commune is the accounting unit, differences are allowed, though the value of a work point is in principle equal. At the beginning of the year each brigade concludes a contract with the commune. This is a "three-fix" contract, i.e. based on the following three points:

1. Total production is set as a target;
2. For fulfilment of each target the brigade is entitled to receive from the commune the value of 100 work points in money;
3. The brigade also receives a certain sum for investment.

At the year's end, the results are examined. If the tasks are fulfilled, the brigade receives the money due under the contract. In case of over-fulfilment, the commune will give extra money, and if the task has not been fulfilled, the value of a work point decreases.

The case of Liuji is particularly interesting inasmuch as it shows that decentralized decision-making enables local organs in China, with the support of the people concerned, to take measures that deviate strikingly from general directives from the centre, provided that the deviation can be convincingly argued.

(3) Liangjiafan

Liangjiafan subcommune in Baiguo commune, Macheng district (Hubei province, to the north of Xinzhou district), also presented some interesting traits in connection with the inequality issue.

Baiguo commune (formerly: subdistrict) comprises nine sub-communes (each formerly a commune), two of which are at present units of account. Among these two is Liangjiafan, already described earlier. In the other seven subcommunes either bri-gades or even production teams are functioning as units of account. Liangjiafan became a unit of account in 1970, when it was still a commune. The system provided several advantages. It greatly facilitated capital construction as well as soil management and the utilization of manpower. For example, there were brigades with excess land and shortage of manpower or the reverse; once combined, they could supplement each other. The system also had good effects for brigades that were unable to make investments: under unified control, investments where poorer brigades were located became possible. Also, thanks to higher production, both in formerly rich and in formerly poor brigades, the value of a work point has been augmented.

The system of concluding contracts with the brigades is similar to that in Liuji commune. Bonuses for brigades exceeding their norms had already existed since 1970 and this was applied before that in the relationship between a brigade and its produc-tion teams. Even today contracts between brigades and teams are being concluded. Mutual services have to be paid for, contrary to the common practice in 1970.

But the power of brigades over teams has decreased; in economic matters actual power is now being exercised by the sub-commune.

It was possible to raise the unit of account in Liangjiafan partly because differences in resources among brigades are not great; in subcommunes where they are greater, it is not allowed.

71

And the government will proceed very cautiously in extending the Liangjiafan experiment. Decisions have to be taken by the members and all experiments need the approval of the province. In this province only six subcommunes are units of account, but the *members* appear to prefer this; they won't wish to go back. It is also favourable for all kinds of enterprises and for the establishment of schools.

In Liangjiafan, about 60 percent of gross income is distributed among the workers. The poorer brigades are either situated in the hills, or in densely populated plains. We paid a visit to the poorest brigade (No.3), situated in the hills, which suffers from a shortage of water and of manure. The irrigation problem has now been solved by the purchase of three pumps (two of them electrical; the rate is 0.08 *yuan* per kw/hour for agriculture, 0.12 for industrial purposes - *much* cheaper than in Tuyuan!).

The poor brigade has received assistance from the subcommune with its water supply and with the installation of electricity. Methane gas, already in use in a rich brigade (No.1), will also be tried out in No.3; the *commune* will pay for it, but labour has to be provided by the brigade, whereas the users themselves have to install the pipes. Poor brigades also receive preference in the establishment of industries. Generally, the custom in Baiguo is to invest a great portion of the profit from its enterprises in poorer units in the hills. The poorer hill areas receive about 90 percent of investment funds; the richer areas only 10 percent. Liangjiafan, being the richest subcommune, does not generally receive assistance from the commune, but if it has an important project, part of the profit can be allocated for this purpose.

The commune also receives assistance from the district (some 300,000 *yuan* annually for agricultural development); it has come regularly since 1960 except that during the Cultural Revolution, the amount was lowered; now it has been raised again. Poorer units are allowed to repay loans later, and at a very low rate of interest (only 0.1 percent per year).

72

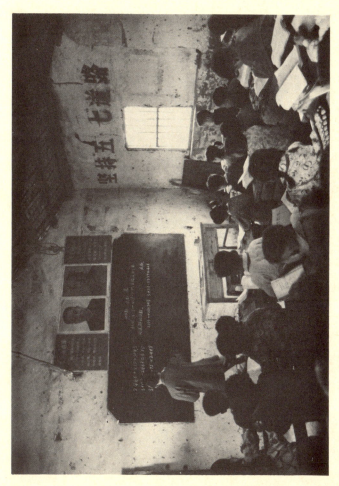

Primary school in Brigade No.3, the poorest brigade of Liangjiafan sub-commune (Hubei).

A final point worth noting is the regular distribution of grain. The granary in brigade No.3 contains a huge quantity of rice in bags and every person (including babies!) receives 40 *jin* (20 kg.) per month.

Consequently, basic needs appear to be catered for in an efficient manner, even in this poorest brigade. The peasants were recently allowed to sell modest quantities of their grain in the free market.

We could therefore conclude that Liangjiafan is not only advanced in production, but also in its policy towards poorer units. Raising the level of the unit of account to commune (later: subcommune) level has substantially contributed to this effect.

(4) *Longchi*

In Longchi commune (Emei district) in the mountains of Sichuan province the production team is still the unit of account which is quite understandable in view of the pronounced differences in level of production among the teams and brigades.

The pattern of income distribution is not uniform for agriculture and for industry (including mining). According to directives from the Central Committee of the Communist Party, not less than 60 percent of gross income is to be distributed among the peasants, while capital accumulation (in this commune, at least) account for no more than 3-5 percent. However, sometimes 60 percent for distribution cannot be attained in some production teams because running expenses have been too high; the worker's share is then reduced and the commune provides assistance to subsidize running expenses. The lowest share distributed in 1978 was 49 percent, as a consequence of a natural calamity, which affected team five of *Taoyuan* brigade. But the peasants' share is augmented by a share in the yield profits of *industrial* enterprises (60 percent of whose gross income is distributed).

Average per capita income in 1978 amounted to 91 *yuan* (over 1979 it would reach about 110 *yuan*) whereas before 1969 it was only 56 *yuan*. The "leap forward" was due mainly to coal mining and medicinal herbs, developed in the seventies. But divergences in income are pronounced.

Average per capita income in the richest production team was 173 *yuan* in 1978, three times higher than in the poorest one (58 *yuan*); and it was twice as high in the richest as in the poorest brigade. But it must be pointed out that the 58-*yuan* average income was earned by a production team high up in the mountains, several hours by foot from the main road as well as from the commune headquarters. One could conclude that the quality of communications might be a key factor in explaining regional inequalities between economic units within a people's commune, and possibly also between neighbouring communes.[1]

---

[1] The following figures give an idea of income differentials between rich and poor production teams and brigades in some of the other communes and counties that we studied in the course of our mission. We were not always able to obtain information on per capita income of economic units; in some cases it was the average income per agricultural labour force, which can be as much as *three times* as high as per capita income. The explanation is that the total value of a unit's production is not divided by the number of inhabitants but by the number of members actually engaged in agricultural production. The following figures, therefore, do not provide a comparison of per capita income between units.

- Macheng county in 1978 (*income per capita*):
  richest unit: 158 *yuan*   = $\frac{2.6}{1}$
  poorest unit: 60 *yuan*

- Liangjiafan subcommune in 1978 (*income per capita*):
  richest unit: 115 *yuan*   = $\frac{1.3}{1}$
  poorest unit: 87 *yuan*

- Liangjiafan subcommune in 1978 (*income per agricultural workforce*):
  richest brigade: 340 *yuan*   = $\frac{1.3}{1}$
  poorest brigade: 254 *yuan*

continued overleaf

There is an interesting system of payment for the hard work
in the commune's coal mine.   For the miners a norm has been
established of 800 kg. of coal per day, which generally amounts to
a work day of five to six hours.   For this work 1.50 *yuan* per day
is paid by the commune to the production team to which the worker
belongs.   He himself gets 0.60 *yuan*; if he exceeds the norm he
gets a bonus.   This regulation has existed since 1968 when for
the first time a brigade started exploiting a coal mine.   (One
year later the mine was taken over by the commune; but since 1970
brigades have also been entitled to exploit coal mines if they
obtain permission from higher authorities.)

Under this system the income of the miner's production team
is not affected by his working in the mine since the team keeps
0.90 *yuan* per day per worker allowed to work in the mine.   A
similar regulation is in force for mines exploited by brigades.
The miners, who generally receive several kinds of supplements in
addition to their 0.60 *yuan* per day, have an income roughly double
that of peasants.

The system is different from the one Wertheim encountered in
commune industries in *Liangzhu* commune (not far from Hangzhou,
Zhejiang province).   There the remuneration of members of an
agricultural production team, who worked in a commune factory, was
calculated in work points whose value was determined by the team's

---

- Tuyuan commune in 1978 (*income per agricultural workforce*):
  richest team: 400 *yuan* $= \dfrac{2.4}{1}$
  poorest team: 170 *yuan*

In extreme cases income differentials between the richest and
poorest units within a commune can reach proportions of 5 or 6
to 1.   In a discussion that Stiefel had with members of the
Commission of Nationalities Affairs in Beijing such a case was
reported to him from Daxin commune (Da'an county, Guangxi autonomous region).   The main reason for such an extreme income
differential seems again to lie in differences in topographical
location and access to communications and services, with the
poorest units being located high up in the mountains.   See also
Appendix II for the calculation of average distribution of
brigade income per person and per labourer.

Workers in the coal mine in Longchi commune have an income roughly double that of peasants.

income, regardless of the output of the factory itself. This meant that workers performing the same work side by side in the same factory might have different incomes.

The state is at present providing some assistance to Longchi commune. For example, until 1978 the commune had to pay five percent of net profit from the mine as a tax; but this obligation was abolished in 1978. Further, poor brigades or teams receive state funds via the Agricultural Bank for installing a pig sty, for example, or for developing the cultivation of a new commercial crop. This assistance takes the form of an interest-free loan from the district, which is distributed by the commune among its teams. An example: one poor team may get five *yuan* per *mou* for reforestation while the commune itself assists with planning and the organization of courses.

From the replies of the commune leadership to our questions regarding the way investments are allocated to different units, we received the impression that this leadership was rather profit-oriented and more interested in "modernization" as such than in how its benefits were distributed. From the 300,000 *yuan* ear-marked for infrastructural works, it appears that only one percent (3,000 *yuan*) was used in areas occupied by the poorest teams for installing electricity; the remainder was used for developing profit-making enterprises, mostly located in the richer units. An example:
- 15,000 *yuan* for buying an electric generator;
- 10,000 *yuan* for broadening a mine gallery, which quad-rupled the daily production;
- 33,000 *yuan* for buying trucks;
- 25,000 *yuan* for irrigation; and the remainder for road building.

It seems very probable that none of these innovations would bene-fit the poorer teams, which were mostly situated up in the mountains.

The commune leaders themselves admitted that assistance to poor teams did not exceed the 3,000 *yuan* mentioned earlier. They pointed out that of the sums borrowed from the state over four to five years, 30,000 *yuan* had not yet been repaid (which might explain their preference for investing in profit-making enterprises). They attributed the weakness of poor teams mainly to "poor leadership", lack of a sense of responsibility, and a conservative way of thinking - and here they were evidently, without realizing it, using a current diagnosis at the time of the "Gang of Four".

We can conclude, therefore, that even if Longchi commune has made appreciable headway since 1970 as far as its "modernization" is concerned, this progress is bound to remain selective favouring only certain aspects of production and benefitting only a limited number of commune members - a type of "progress" well-known in many other Third World countries. This type of selective growth is bound to remain permanent unless the push for high production is combined with an emphasis on fair income distribution. It should be noted, by the way, that Longchi is *for a mountain commune* an exceptionally *rich* one, and thus not entirely representative of mountain communes in China.

Moreover, we were hardly impressed by the way "modern machinery" in the shape of motor transport was actually used in this region. During our stay in Emei district we saw four or five trucks or tractors that had been wrecked, it was clear, due to their drivers' negligence. The reaction of onlookers was gaiety rather than sorrow at the squandering of so much collective or state property by carelessness or incompetence. If poor brigades or mountain teams had received some of the mules they so badly need they would probably take better care of them.

A final point related to the inequality issue in Sichuan province: in 1974/1975 country-wide discussion took place to decide which unit should manage the tractor stations. It was decided that the people's commune rather than the district should own and manage the tractors and that, in the case of smaller tractors, the brigade may be the suitable unit.   At present, it seems, there are no plans to shift the management unit to the district level; moveover, it is felt that if this happened the relationship between the state and collective property and management might create serious problems.

There is keen competition among communes for too small a number of tractors available and the criteria for obtaining priority present a problem.   Allocations are decided by the prefecture and district administrations, according to considerations of *urgency*.   However, in answer to our question as to how urgency was determined, the reply was that people's communes able to *pay* without borrowing received preference.   This hardly seemed an appropriate way to combat inequality.

There are some signs that, quite recently, the party leadership may be becoming aware of the dangers of too great a stress on the "enrich yourselves" policy.   In the *People's Daily* of 17 January 1980, a leading article was published under the title "Show concern for backward areas: help communes and production brigades and teams in difficulty".   The article argues that although it is essential that emphasis is given to areas, communes, production brigades and teams that have relatively good conditions in order to allow them to become rich as soon as possible, there is "another task facing us" which "cannot be overlooked *and is far more urgent*.   We should also make great efforts to help communes and production brigades and teams who are in difficulty - and there are quite a few of them - to quickly eliminate their backwardness and (make them) gradually catch up with the rich ones".   And the newspaper adds: "If production in these areas cannot be accelerated and the masses' enthusiasm raised, the overall pace of agricultural growth will be affected".   The article notes that in a quarter of the production teams throughout the country collective production is now in poor shape, and that most of the disadvantaged places where members live very hard lives are in remote and mountainous areas.

Leaders in party and state departments at all levels are urged to allow and encourage certain communes, brigades, teams and their members "to get rich first, and then let the poor units learn from their experiences". In addition practical measures were needed "to help them (the poor units) analyse the causes of their poverty and lead them to advance toward prosperity."

In order to achieve this, in addition to teaching them "primarily to rely on the efforts of the local people", the state must "still give them financial and material support" since they have "weak foundations".[1] The article stated that "in 1979, the state exempted low-income communes and production brigades and teams from agricultural taxes and their enterprises from industrial and commercial taxes, thus creating favourable conditions for developing their production and restoring their energy". But because of an impossibility for China "to allocate still more money to help them", strict supervision is essential "to ensure the correct use of the limited funds for poor production brigades and teams".

The article concludes with an admonition that the issue is related to "the mass viewpoint and class feeling that every communist should have", and that leading comrades at all levels should "always bear in mind the suffering of the masses" and "show concern for backward areas".[2]

---

[1] The same concern for assisting poorer units in mountain areas also emerged from a conference of the Sichuan Provincial Party Committee on new policies for these areas. It was decided to relax economic policy restrictions for poor brigades in the less-developed mountain areas by reducing grain quotas or even providing subsidized grain, giving financial help for the construction of roads and small hydro-electric stations, and providing more generous long-term low-interest loans, *SWB*, FE/W1104/A/11, 15 October 1980.

[2] All quotations from *People's Daily* article, 17 January 1980.

Should we consider this publication as a new turning point in Chinese agrarian strategy, which would imply that egalitarian ideas are to be stressed more than in the recent past?   Though some indications can be found in this publication, we have not yet encountered any evidence that it could be interpreted as foreboding a real reorientation in rural strategies.   But it is gratifying to note, on the one hand, that an excessive stress on "relying on one's own forces", prevalent during the Cultural Revolution, is now definitely being rejected, and that on the other hand the "enrich yourselves" slogan is now recognized as unsatisfactory to achieve balanced progress.

It would be interesting to find out, however, to what extent this sudden stress on the specific needs of backward areas might be due to feelings of discontent expressed by peasants living in these under-privileged areas.

If education in "the thought of Mao Zedong" during the past three decades had any effect on the peasant masses, it seems quite plausible that those living in poor areas or units would begin to move, in order to claim their share of the "four modernizations". Such expressions of dissatisfaction would also represent one way of "relying on one's own forces".

—————————o0o—————————

PART III

PARTICIPATION AND HIERARCHY

A. <u>Historical Outline</u>

The Chinese Socialist Revolution was based on a large-scale participation of the peasants in the revolutionary struggle; as such, it was in itself a basically participatory process carried forward by the release of spontaneous forces of broad rural masses liberated from the traditional social control. However, as with all revolutions, the Chinese revolution was not led by peasants, but by "minorities of defectors from the élite" organized in the form of the Communist Party, as Lucien Bianco had called it. The Chinese Communist Party mobilized peasant participation by combining identification with the peasants' aspirations with organization and indoctrination. From the outset the germs of a possible contradiction between party authority and broad-based mass participation were present; they became apparent once the party assumed power in 1949 and was faced with the task of actually institutionalizing popular participation in the revolution, taking into account the strong power of local rural communities.

The Chinese revolutionary process, after initially starting and being crushed in industrial centres like Shanghai, Guangzhou and Wuhan, took refuge in the countryside; thus it did not successfully spread from an industrial capital to the countryside and to the periphery, as happened in 1917 and the following years in Russia. On the contrary, the Communist movement established a number of strong guerrilla bases in the interior and only in a final phase conquered the larger urban centres. Consequently, the logical outcome was a considerable amount of decentralization.

After the Chinese People's Republic had been established in 1949, with a unified Communist Party in command, many relics of the early revolutionary phase, including a significant measure of regional and local autonomy, remained. This was to a large extent due to the enormous area of the country, and to great differences in geographic situation and in way of life related to climatic conditions and cultural traditions. But it was not until 1958 that a certain decentralization within the government apparatus would develop a concrete form, with the creation of people's communes. It is worth remembering that the idea of strong local communities as a counterweight to a centralized bureaucracy is not new to China; it has even sometimes been claimed that Mao took this idea from Chinese 17th century philosophers.

The advanced cooperatives formed in 1956/1957 only functioned in the realm of the rural economy: they did not possess any general governing or administrative functions, which were still fully vested in the lowest units of the state hierarchy. Mostly this lowest level of government administration was represented by the *xiang* (township), which functioned as a unit of rural administration. (During 1955-1957 many townships were merged into new units called "big townships", *da xiang*, encompassing several cooperatives.)

When Wertheim visited the People's Republic for the first time in 1957, he was struck by the existence in the countryside of a kind of double administration. When he visited a rural cooperative, representatives of both the governing board of the *xiang* and of the executive board of the cooperative were present. Questions regarding agriculture were answered by the chairman or chairwoman of the co-op; but whenever he touched upon problems of sideline production or population figures, the replies were given by *xiang* representatives. A merger of the two parallel administrations into one was therefore quite logical.

In the people's commune, economic cooperation in agriculture and sideline production were combined with the lowest level of government administration. The principles of collective ownership of land and collective land use considerably strengthened the autonomous power of these focal units of rural administration. Henceforth, the people's commune not only coordinated the activities of the lower units (brigades, generally congruous with a natural village and originating from advanced cooperatives, which in their turn coordinated the work of production teams, mostly congruous with hamlets); it also acquired a certain bargaining power in its relations with higher administrative units: the *xian* (county) and the province. The people's communes were still formally subordinated to these higher levels of administration and had to draw up their plans in accordance with the general planning at national, provincial or county level. But planning in China is generally conceived as a two-way process: the final plan is drawn up only after the original drafts have gone up and down the hierarchical line, which means that consultation with the lower levels is not just a pure formality.

As well as the higher levels of the state administration, there was another unifying factor in Chinese rural policies: the Chinese Communist Party, providing political leadership and general ideological guidance. The Central Committee was entitled to issue general directives, also in connection with economic policies and rural strategies. These were transmitted from the top down to the different levels of the party organization. Since the party was represented at each intermediate level by party committees down to the basic level of the people's commune, there was a strong pressure that all kinds of concrete decisions at the local level would conform with the general line adopted by the central party organs. We have to bear in mind that wherever executives at different levels are responsible to elected bodies, the decisions these bodies take are again strongly influenced by the party line as established by the top level and transmitted to the party committees at the lower level.

85

To provide a direct link with the masses, the party established a number of *mass organizations*, such as the Youth League,
the Women's Federation or the Association of Poor and Lower Middle
Peasants, whose function was to serve as a transmission belt between the party organs and the masses.   It was their task to explain party guidelines to the people and obtain their adherence to
these guidelines.

For the issue of popular participation, two guiding principles of the Chinese governing style are of crucial importance.
These principles concern, first, the role and the work of the
Communist Party and have been clearly defined in the Party Rules,
adopted at the (8th) Party Congress in 1956.   For intra-party relationships "democratic centralism" is the leading principle,
whereas for relations between the party and the people the "mass
line" is a basic concept.

"Democratic centralism" is a concept coined by Lenin and refers to the operation of a communist party as such.   It means
that within a communist party decisions have to be arrived at by
democratic consultation, but that once a decision has been taken
by a central organ it has to be followed in a disciplined way, regardless of personal views, and without allowing factions to arise
within the party.

In China "democratic centralism" has been used in a somewhat
different sense.   To quote Franz Schurmann:

> "...the Chinese Communists have broken the old Leninist term
> 'democratic centralism' into two component nominal units,
> democracy *and* centralism, and in their dialectical fashion,
> have juxtaposed the two... The Chinese Communists have never
> advocated instituting democracy at the full expense of cen-
> tralism, but rather a system which combined the two in a
> unity of true opposites."[1]

---

[1] Franz Schurmann, *Ideology and Organization in Communist China*,
2nd ed. Berkeley, 1968, pp.86/87.

According to Schurmann the Chinese have, in other words, always been aware of "the contradiction between centralism and democracy, and between center and region"; this may also explain why their general type of policy took the form of a "downward transfer of authority to the regional level".

It should be noted, however, that whereas the dualist interpretation of "democratic centralism" as defined by Schurmann belongs to the Maoist tradition, in publications by Liu Shaoqi decidedly more stress was laid on party discipline, as for example in his book (authoritative at the time of the 8th Party Congress), *How to Be a Good Communist*.

The other aspect of party principles related to the concept of democracy, which seems of still greater importance for our issue of popular participation as applicable to rural society, is the "mass line" concept. It was first enunciated by Mao, in a directive announced from Yan-an on June 1, 1943:

> "All correct leadership is necessarily from the masses, to the masses. This means: take the ideas of the masses (scattered and unsystematic ideas) and concentrate them (through study turn them into concentrated and systematic ideas), then go to the masses and propagate and explain these ideas until the masses embrace them as their own, hold fast to them and translate them into action, and test the correctness of these ideas in such action."[1]

The principle has been confirmed in the Party Rules adopted at the 8th Party Congress. To quote Schurmann again:

> "The theme that runs through the General Outline (of the Party Rules) as well as through the whole 8th Party Congress is the mass line. The party must get closer to the masses, imbed itself in them. This was proclaimed explicitly as the Party's policy line for the years to come."[2]

---

[1] Stuart R. Schram, "Introduction: The Cultural Revolution in Historical Perspective", in Stuart R. Schram (ed.) *Authority, Participation and Cultural Change in China*, Cambridge, 1973, p.29.

[2] Franz Schurmann, *op.cit.*, p.126.

The "mass line" and "democratic centralism", two guiding principles of Chinese politics, imply regular meetings between cadres and peasants at all levels. Above: meeting of Production Team Leaders and Chairman of Brigade No.1, Liangjiafan subcommune (Hubei).

In a later discussion of the term "democratic centralism", Mao combined this concept with the "mass line" principle in such a manner that "democratic centralism" no longer remained restricted to intra-Party relationships, but also included relations of the party with the masses. Mao argued in his speech to 7,000 cadres in January 1962:

> "In short we can only use democratic methods, the method of letting the masses speak out. Both inside and outside the party, there must be full democratic life, which means conscientiously putting democratic centralism into effect."[1]

As defined by Mao "democratic centralism", integrated with the "mass line" concept, has thus been largely disengaged from what Stuart Schram calls the "élitist" origins in the Leninist interpretations of "Party democracy".[2]

A significant element in the Chinese governing style was that, in attempting to achieve a behaviour of the people in conformity with the general party line advocated by the central party organs, stress was laid on education and persuasion rather than on compulsion. For example, a directive issued by Mao on 1 October 1943, regarding land reforms stated that they were not to be introduced by decree but through a struggle waged in each village separately by the peasants, once they had overcome their original fear of the landlords' power by means of a prolonged mass education campaign by the Poor Peasants' Organizations.

Shortly after the birth of the Chinese People's Republic, Zhou Enlai expressed himself in a similar way, referring to Mao's

---

[1] See e.g. Joost B.W. Kuitenbrouwer, *Rural Transformation in China*, The Hague, 1979, p.18. Mao concluded his talk with the following words: "The aim is to make people unafraid in their hearts and to let them express their opinions... When you have gone back, you must build up democratic centralism."

[2] Stuart Schram, *op.cit.*, pp.28/29.

concept of democracy.   In a report from 1949 he approvingly described Mao's working style as follows:

> "What is to be done when the leadership's correct ideas
> are not accepted by the people?   The answer is we must wait
> and do some persuading.   But, when the great majority do
> not agree, we must follow the majority organizationally...
> This means that very often the view of the leadership will
> triumph and become acceptable after many twists and turns
> and a period of waiting."

The "correct ideas" can be transformed into a strength of
the people, however,

> "...this cannot be accomplished by rashness, but needs great
> perseverance and patience so as to push the revolution for-
> ward with tenacity and win final victory."1/

During Wertheim's second visit to China in 1964, when he was
able to visit ten people's communes as well as some state farms,
he noticed several times that persuasion was still being considered the only correct manner to get things done.   For example,
when he asked why *not all* the children went to school, the reply
was: "We do not wish to compel the children if they really do not
want to go.   What we try is to speak with the children as well as
with the parents, and to attempt to persuade them to return to
school."   Of course Wertheim was aware that in actual practice
strong moral pressure from the whole social environment was often
difficult to distinguish from compulsion.   For example, in order
to obtain the general cooperation of the people in all kinds of
campaigns (e.g. for construction of hydraulic works, or in connection with the *xiafang* movement, i.e. persuading urban youth to go
"up to the mountains or down to the villages").

In some talks he had with local cadres, they tried to make
clear that penal sanctions (for example, for neglecting rules of
cleanliness) were much less effective than mass education.   This

---

1/ See *Peking Review* 27/10/1978 (No.43).

was the main reason why legal provisions were kept at a minimum. The underlying assumption was that a positive approach towards human beings, considered as essentially educable, is in the long run a much more effective one than legal provisions and sanctions. In this respect, the Maoist way of thinking was not much different from Confucian ethics, which also put stress on the educability of man.

It would be useful to inject here a few words about the formal structure of authority within the people's communes, as it was before the Cultural Revolution. Benedict Stavis gives the following description:

> "As with the team and brigade, the commune has a members' congress of representatives. The representatives are elected for two-year terms, and are supposed to meet twice a year. The representatives are supposed to include representatives of all interests in the commune. This includes members in various occupations, experienced old peasants, rural specialized workers, youth, women, members belonging in minority nationalities, members of martyrs' families, demobilized soldiers, members of overseas Chinese families, intellectuals, and returned overseas Chinese. These representatives are elected by the brigade congress, but the commune Party Committee plays an important role in nominating the representatives to the commune congress."

> "The commune congress elects the commune director, other members of the management committee, and the supervisory committee. Their term of office is two years, and they may be elected for successive terms."

> "Before the Cultural Revolution, the process of selection of commune leaders was dominated by the county Party Committee. It would make suggestions to the commune congress for managers and directors, and the commune congress would generally simply approve. The process was tantamount to having commune leaders appointed by the county level.[1]

One of the main objectives of the Cultural Revolution was to reinforce popular control of cadres. Through an open critique of cadres and institutions the people were to become more assertive

---

[1] Benedict Stavis, *People's Communes and Rural Development in China*, Ithaca, N.Y., rev. 2nd ed., 1977, p.106 and 107.

91

in order to break authoritarian relations of control that were
again predominant and to oppose bureaucratic practices, both
within the Communist Party and within the government. The principle of *consultation of the masses* was still upheld, even more
strongly than before, at least in theory. At Wertheim's third
visit (1970/1971) he even noticed that the idea of long-term
planning was rejected. Though annual or five-year plans were
still being drafted, the Chinese opposed future projections, which
were becoming popular in the West. When Wertheim asked a foreign
expert who had lived for decades in China why the Chinese did not
envisage a surplus of manpower as soon as mechanization of agriculture actually got under way he was told:

> "You do not understand the way the Chinese are proceed-
> ing. They are not 'planning for the year 2000' as you pre-
> tend to do in the West, which largely amounts to building
> castles in the air. They keep nearer to the ground. Now
> and then one of their leaders, maybe Mao himself, travels
> around the country. Whenever he sees a local initiative,
> which in his view is a good solution to some concrete prob-
> lems, the example is published and popularised in the Press.
> In this way also the people's communes came to life."1/

This reply seemed in accordance with the main principles of
the "mass line": "from the masses to the masses".

The formal structure of authority within people's communes
underwent certain changes during the Cultural Revolution. Stavis
first mentions some changes in nomenclature:

> "The Commune Management Committee is now called the
> Commune Revolutionary Committee. The title of Commune
> Director (*she-chang*) has been transformed to Chairman of the
> Revolutionary Committee."

He then goes on:

1/ W.F. Wertheim, "Rainbow Bridge Commune Revisited", 2nd part,
Eastern Horizon, Vol.11, No.1, 1972, p.40.

"After the Cultural Revolution, the process of leadership selection was democratized.   More mass discussions and
consultations take place in the selection of delegates to
brigade and commune congresses.   Secondly, the leading and
responsible cadres at each level are no longer nominated by
higher authorities.   They are elected by their own level.
Thus, even with the democratization of the Cultural Revolution, the higher levels continue to exercise considerable
influence over selection of leaders and can make sure that
no one who opposes the basic communist policies can exercise
formal leadership."1/

However, Stavis admits that the precise institutional arrangements involved in electing the Commune Revolutionary Committee are not clear and probably vary from place to place.
Wertheim noticed in 1970/1971 that, with the restoration of party
organization and party committees at different levels, the Revolutionary Committees became again subordinated to party supervision.
It is, therefore, likely that a remarkable measure of autonomy,
which the commune had been able to acquire during the years of
turmoil (1967/1968), has become weaker since.   At the 9th Party
Congress (1969), the party gradually regained its former power. It
is possible, however, that at the time when the party was not
functioning smoothly, the Army had temporarily taken over the
ideological leadership.

Another aspect of the Cultural Revolution worth mentioning
in connection with the formal structures in the countryside is
leadership according to the principle of three-in-one, adopted in
1967 as the guiding principle for the composition of Revolutionary
Committees in general.   For the people's communes, this probably
implied that care was taken within each Revolutionary Committee
that at least three categories were represented: the cadres, the
masses and the militia.   Within the Party Committees also the
principle of three-in-one was adopted; but here the triad rather
referred to a composition in which old, middle-aged and young members were all represented.   An important feature was a strong

---

1/ Benedict Stavis, op.cit., p.107.

93

personal union between the two committees.   For example, the
Secretary of the Party Committee of the people's commune was
usually also Chairman of the Revolutionary Committee.

In the present criticism of the Cultural Revolution this
period is being labelled as one in which arbitrary rule prevailed
and democratic elections were all but eliminated.   Though all
kinds of excesses may have actually occurred, it is difficult to
believe that practice was so much at variance with declared
principles.   During his third trip to China (1970/1971) Wertheim
was struck several times in people's communes with an increased
awareness of collective interests among the peasants.   He wrote
in *Eastern Horizon*:[1]

> "After having visited several communes I tend to con-
> firm the claim, generally heard, that since the Cultural
> Revolution the awareness of collective interest and a trend
> to delay immediate consumption in favour of building for the
> future, has spread towards broader layers of the rural popu-
> lation.   I do not assert that before 1964 this type of
> social consciousness was altogether lacking; but a trend
> which was already discernible before that time has been
> appreciably strengthened since."

As examples of this trend he mentioned a new tendency among brigades to lend their "most capable and progressive workers out to a
backward brigade", and the preparedness of brigades with fertile
soil to let neighbouring brigades fetch clods of clay for mixing
it with their sandy soils, without any pay.   On that visit he was
also shown projects said to have been accomplished by peasants
without any expert supervision, among them "a stone bridge with
seven bows", in *Dongfeng* commune near Guangzhou.   But he added in
his report: "To what extent the stories, as told to me, are true
to life and not mere embellished illustrations of a cherished
stereotype was difficult to check."

---

[1] *Eastern Horizon*, Vol.11, No.1, 1972.

During our visit in 1979 it was difficult to get confirmation of these positive trends in the early years of the Cultural Revolution, as far as popular participation was concerned. In recollections of that period stress was rather laid on the anarchic tendencies of those years, and on the impossibility for many cadres to provide the required leadership. However, in an indirect way a certain confirmation could be obtained: the energetic collective activities developed during those years, according to our informants, for example in initiating all kinds of infrastructural works, all indicate such an increased awareness of collective interest - even more so if, as we were told, the cadres had actually lost part of their authority!

When Wertheim reminded them of his personal experiences in 1970/1971 the cadres who accompanied us in 1979 tended to say: "But at that time they were lying to you!" As for the stone bridge in Dongfeng commune, he was able to check this out. The story he got this time about the way the bridge had been constructed in the early years of the Cultural Revolution tallied exactly with the story he had been told in 1970 and which at *that* time seemed to him a bit fantastic.

We might conclude that the Cultural Revolution led to a lasting raising of consciousness but that there were also outbursts of anarchy that sometimes led to excesses and to arbitrary rule.

B. <u>Recent Developments and Present Trends</u>

Since Mao's death great changes have occurred in the formulation of basic policies and short- and long-term social and economic objectives, and the "four modernizations" are posited as principal task. However, a modern, increasingly complex economic system, as the present Chinese leaders envisage, requires conditions of great stability and regularity, and this has strongly influenced Chinese concepts of democracy. Whereas at the time of the Cultural Revolution management of all kinds of organizations was formally put into the hands of elected "Revolutionary Committees", the new policies adopted since 1977 again stress the strengthening of managerial powers. Particularly in state industry, a stricter discipline was reintroduced in order to promote a rapid rise in production and a successful implementation of the programme of "four modernizations". In spite of the new trend to increase managerial powers and enforce stricter discipline, the new policies are officially presented as a return to democratic practices.

This strengthening of managerial powers is accompanied by a *real transfer of decision-making and responsibilities* from the state and higher collective units to individual production units (enterprises, teams, etc.). To this extent there is increased participation of these units (this is what the Chinese call "self-management"), however the participation of the workers and peasants *within* the production units tends to decrease because of the extension of managerial powers. Also, this relative "democratization" seems to be introduced for purely utilitarian and not ideological reasons. It is denied that at the time of the Cultural Revolution (including the seventies) democracy prevailed. Instead of promoting "popular participation", the role of "Lin Biao and the Gang of Four" would have led to compulsion and arbitrary rule.

Whereas throughout the Cultural Revolution *informal* methods of consultation of the people were stressed, according to the new policy democratic forms have to be *institutionalized*. It is the 1978 Constitution (5th National People's Congress) that laid the provisions for a *complete new legal system*.

According to the present Chinese leaders, the fight against bureaucratic hypertrophy, abuses and power has not been discontinued after the Cultural Revolution, only the means of fighting it have changed. While during the Cultural Revolution the masses were mobilized to constitute *de facto* a countervailing power to the bureaucracy, it is now legal institutions and regulations that provide a check on the bureaucracy. *Legal* guarantees and regulations are now advocated and gradually introduced in order to ensure that decisions at all levels are taken according to prescribed procedures and not by arbitrary rule. Whereas, according to the concepts prevalent during Mao's life, legal provisions were to be kept to a minimum, and behaviour in accordance with the general strategy was largely considered a matter of patient education of the people, now great reliance is placed on legal provisions.

From official publications and the Chinese press one sometimes gets the impression that the Chinese authorities tend now towards the opposite extreme: as though they consider a matter as settled as soon as the required legal provisions have been introduced. They seem to overlook that laws and regulations, having been formulated, have first to be interpreted and adapted to local circumstances before they can actually be applied and enforced, and that observance of laws and regulations and the way they are applied depends to a large extend on patient education, both of the authorities entrusted with enforcing the law and of the people. Moreover, application of laws in accordance with general strategies has to be controlled - and here we are again confronted with the universal issue: who will "keep the keepers"?

It seems evident, taking into account experiences elsewhere in the world, that legal provisions as such can never provide a foolproof guarantee for observance of general rules and norms of behaviour. Putting managerial powers into the hands of a bureaucratic élite creates a danger of authoritarian and arbitrary rule. Popular control of the way laws and regulations are implemented remains a precondition for actual popular participation in any decision-making process.

Therefore, it remains important to assess the present views in China regarding the two aspects of popular participation mentioned above: "democratic centralism" and the "mass line".

As we have seen, the term "democratic centralism" stems from Lenin and generally refers to relationships and procedures *within* a Communist Party. We have seen that "democratic centralism" as interpreted by Liu Shaoqi laid specific stress on party discipline once a decision had been reached by democratic discussions among party members or within the party leadership. It is not surprising that after Mao's death the concept is still acknowledged as a leading principle of party life, but that at the same time it seems to have undergone a return to the Leninist interpretation.

While democratic consultation inside the party is upheld, great stress is again laid on the obligation of all party organs "to implement the party's resolutions and to observe its discipline".[1] A Central Commission for Inspecting Discipline was established in December 1978 by the Party Central Committee, to be assisted by party discipline inspection commissions of all levels in the task of upholding party discipline and work style.[2] The concept "democratic centralism" seems no longer to be used in connection with relationships between the party and the popular masses, as Mao had advocated in 1962.

The "mass line" is still repeatedly referred to in Chinese newspapers and other publications.[3] One nevertheless gets the impression that in spite of a verbal adherence to this principle, it has lost a good deal of its relevance in actual policies, at least at the central level and in juridical procedures. This is probably due partly to all kinds of irregularities and excesses

---

[1] See, for example, an article in the *People's Daily*, 21/7/1980, under the title "Learn from Lenin, strengthen the Party's democratic centralism".

[2] *Beijing Review*, No.14, 6 April 1979.

[3] The "mass line" has been reconfirmed, for example, as an "essential way to map out our long-term programme" in Hua Guofeng's speech on 7 September 1980, at the 3rd session of the 5th National People's Congress (see *Beijing Review*, 22/9/1980, No.38).

that were committed during the seventies in the name of the "mass line".

For example, in the Constitution of 1975 (article 25, paragraph 3) it was stipulated that in matters of prosecution and accusation, as well as in trials, the "mass line" had to be applied. In principle, such a provision could ensure an extensive measure of popular control over criminal procedures. But it is evident that in actual practice public opinion could be manipulated by power-holders on a local level in a way detrimental to a correct administration of justice.

In the Constitution of 1978, adopted at the 5th National People's Congress, the "mass line" as such is no longer mentioned. However, article 41 still stipulates that "with regard to major counter-revolutionary or criminal cases, the masses should be drawn in for discussion and suggestions". Moreover, in the people's courts "representatives of the masses participate as assessors in administering justice". Further, it is stipulated that "all cases in the people's courts are heard in public except those involving special circumstances as prescribed by law".

From the foregoing one could deduce that, as far as popular control of criminal procedures is concerned, there is no complete break with the system embodied in the Constitution of 1975. However, at present much more stress is laid on *legal* guarantees. The introduction of a Penal Code and of a Code of Criminal Practice is symptomatic of this new general trend.

One could easily get the impression that the new policies, with their increased stress on discipline (both within the Communist Party and within economic units, as for example industrial enterprises), would result in a generally less democratic atmosphere, with a decrease in popular participation. We may note that in 1977 and 1978, after the fall of the "Gang", there was a short period of democratic liberalization (similar to the "Hundred Flowers" period), at least in urban areas, which seems to have been pushed by rehabilitated intellectuals and urban youth.

But since 1979 there has been a strong repression of this democratic opposition and criticism. What the party leadership apparently wants is a *well-ordered society, in which "democracy" is allowed for utilitarian reasons but is carefully controlled and shaped in order to reinforce and stabilize the regime*, as a precondition for efficient management and for carrying through the "four modernizations".

The impression that democratic atmosphere and popular participation have been severely restricted is reinforced by the recent decision at the 5th National Congress to delete the section in article 45 of the Constitution of 1978 (already present in 1975 version) allowing citizens to "speak out freely, air their views fully, hold great debates and write big-character posters". The official argument for this deletion was that these "Four Freedoms" had been abused to accuse many people falsely, that slander should be combated, and that there remain enough possibilities for the people to express themselves.

The present leadership and the Chinese press would certainly deny that the changes of the past few years amount to a decrease in democratic rights. On the contrary, they claim that the radical changes are intended to safeguard enjoyment of democratic rights by all citizens and to protect them for arbitrary rule. The period of the Cultural Revolution and its aftermath is being presented as one during which anarchy reigned and which enabled local despots to grasp power under the pretence of representing the voice of the masses. The new policies aim at ensuring democratic rights by *legal* provisions, and by granting the right of free, direct and secret elections. The absolute domination of the Communist Party has also been formally impaired, by granting the right to elect candidates for local, regional or national congresses from outside the party. *Formally*, there is a return to the situation that prevailed before the Cultural Revolution, when political parties in addition to the Communist Party were officially granted the right to exist and to participate in elections.

On the other hand, one may ask whether these *formal* freedoms will contribute to retaining, at the local level, the element of direct democracy and popular participation typical of the People's Republic of China in earlier decades. Most important, even basic, is the question of whether, and if so to what extent, direct democracy and popular participation are reconcilable with "the four modernizations". Is increase in size of economic units, which is generally concomitant with modernization and with progressive mechanization of the means of production, compatible with a large measure of consultation with the masses? The same question could be asked about technological sophistication in production, which calls for experts and technicians "who know better than the masses". And, most important of all, can this principle of consulting the masses be retained in an economic system that stresses speedy developments and sets fixed targets for all kinds of material achievements?

C. Experiences during UNRISD mission

Even during the first briefing by his hosts in Beijing, Wertheim was struck by the great stress laid on *legal* provisions to deal with all kinds of problems. Questions about industrial pollution, or about advances in reforestation since his last visit, were not answered by citing concrete achievements but by referring to laws in the making - as though legislation guaranteed correct implementation.

General discussions on "democracy" showed that as far back as autumn 1979 the so-called "Democratic Wall" in Beijing, which offered freedom to attach "big-character posters", was giving the leadership some misgivings. The very term "Democratic Wall" was an invention of foreign journalists, and was not used by the Chinese themselves, we were told. Our hosts observed that a much more important democratic right was to have letters to the editor published in Chinese newspapers, already a widely-used manner of expressing complaints or criticisms that could reach a wider audience, whereas the *dazibaos* on the "Democratic Wall" could only be read by people in Beijing.   When Wertheim retorted that published "Letters to the Editor" had probably been subjected to selection and censorship by the editorial board and therefore could not be equated with the freedom to write and attach "big-character posters", it was pointed out that the anonymity of *dazibaos* was considered a deviation from true democratic procedures[1], because the writer could thus lodge complaints in an irresponsible way.

In Shanghai, Wertheim gathered information of some relevance to the issue of democratic rights.   In the prison he saw a blackboard on which a series of names appeared, followed by ratings ranging from about 70 to 90.   He was told the ratings referred to a special prisoners' study group formed to examine the new Penal Code and the Code of Criminal Practice due to be enacted early in 1980.   These prisoners were able to learn about their rights towards the wardens and other prison officials and could lodge complaints if they were treated in ways that contravened the regulations about to be enacted.

Since there were many young people among the prisoners, it could be assumed that criminality in Shanghai was on the increase as a consequence of the too-hasty return of hundreds of thousands of young people who had "voluntarily" enlisted to go "up to the mountains or down to the villages".   Given the massive return of these people to Shanghai as soon as they were legally able to do so, it seemed likely that either the voluntary nature of their stay in the countryside was questionable or their stay in the countryside had so disappointed them that they craved for a return to city life.

---

[1] This argument in favour of formally abolishing "the four big freedoms" in the Constitution has also been used in *Beijing Review*, No.40, 6/10/1980, ("Rise and Fall of 'Dazibao'"), pp. 22 ff.

The way the Cultural Revolution affected the relationship between commune leaders and their members, as well as the general atmosphere in rural China, varied appreciably from place to place. For example, in one commune (Liangzhu) in Zhejiang province, which Wertheim had visited both in 1964 and in 1970/1971, remarkable progress has been achieved since 1971, with full cooperation of the commune members, in raising and diversifying production. But during the years 1974-1976 a bad influence had been exerted by a prominent authority in Zhejiang province, Wen Xinhe, described as a staunch supporter of the "Gang of Four", who was allegedly against attempts to raise production on behalf of "a wrong line". Consequently, both popular participation and efforts by commune members to develop grain production had decreased for several years.[1]

On the other hand, in *Renhe* commune, not far from Guangzhou, which Wertheim visited in 1970/1971 as well as in 1979[2], the "Gang of Four" were said to have exerted hardly any influence at all. When Wertheim asked the chairman of the Revolutionary Committee, whom he had already met in 1970, whether there had not been any difficulties in 1975/1976, he replied: "Yes, in 1975 we had heavy typhoons, and consequently we lost some 10 percent of our harvest. But as far as 1976 is concerned - no, there were no particular hardships." Wertheim's interpreter, who understood quite well what he was after, asked explicitly: "But didn't you suffer from the influence of the Gang of Four?" The reply was:

---

[1] For a detailed discussion of Liangzhu commune we may refer to W.F. Wertheim, "L'économie rurale en Chine - Dix années perdues?", *Revue des Pays de l'Est*, Vol.21, No.1, 1980, pp.139 ff. The nefarious role of Wen Xinhe in Zhejiang province during the reign of the "Gang of Four", particularly in connection with industry, is also mentioned in Govind Kelkar, *China after Mao: A Report on Socialist Development*, New Delhi, 1979, pp.137/138.

[2] In 1970 the name of *Renhe* (Harmony) commune had been changed to *Dongfeng* (East Wind) commune, but by 1979 the commune had again taken up its original name of *Renhe*.

"No, here in the countryside it did not really affect us. There was a *slight* decrease in grain production." Later on he said that reforestation efforts by the commune members had been slowed down during the seventies. On the other hand, a huge dam with flood-gates had been built during the same period, which had transformed "Disaster River" into what was now called "River of Happiness".

It was only during our in-depth field study farther inland that we could attempt to penetrate somewhat deeper into the aspect of people's participation as an element in Chinese rural strategies before, during and after the Cultural Revolution.

Since our mission was conceived mainly as a kind of feasibility study we attempted first to discover what kind of methods could be used to investigate the role of popular participation as an element of rural strategies. In accordance with our original research project we tried at first to find out whether it would be possible to regard the type of research undertaken by us as primarily historical.[1] Our starting point was that we had to try to assess to what extent the people concerned had actually contributed towards all kinds of crucial decisions, particularly since the establishment of the people's communes (in 1958). We had decided that for this purpose it would be necessary not only to interview cadres but also ordinary peasants. In principle, the best method would have been to interview individual peasants, without any cadres present, to avoid the risk that the respondents' replies would be tinged with official interpretations of past events; but such an arrangement would have required a longer stay in one place. For example, in Tuyuan commune (Guangdong province) we were able to interview individual peasants in the brigade

---

[1] In the original research proposal we had suggested to apply primarily a historical approach because we felt that the present political struggles could make a study of recent policies difficult. *Democratic Centralism and the Mass Line in Rural Chine - an assessment of the Chinese experience in popular participation*, UNRISD/79/C.24, June 1979.

office; however, not only were some brigade and commune leaders all the time present, but we also needed their help, because our official interpreters had difficulties in understanding the local dialect. Nevertheless, our historical approach provided us with important general information about the way popular participation occurred in the past.

Whenever we came across important innovations (as, for example, construction of a big dam plus reservoir in 1958/1959; raising the level of the unit of account; introduction of a new crop; or exploitation by a brigade or commune of a coal mine) we attempted to find out by questioning different people how the innovation had come about. Our general impression was that, in most cases, the new ideas had arisen first among the local leader-ship, or had been suggested by some outside adviser (an engineer, perhaps, in the service of the province or county). We hardly came across any case where the idea had emerged from the masses themselves, as is implied in Mao's concept "from the masses to the masses". Where the masses generally came in, however, was in giving form and substance to the new idea. Often there seemed to have been an appreciable time lag between the moment when the new idea had first been launched and its actual implementation. When we attempted to find out why an interval of many years had elapsed, it usually emerged that no decision was taken until the leadership had made sure that the large majority of the people involved agreed. Popular participation, in these cases, actually boiled down to a type of "mobilization"; but we became convinced that in general care was taken to consult members of the collective unit and that no decisive steps would be taken unless there was suf-ficient evidence that the people concerned would support the decision.

Of course, the interests of different groups of members often conflicted. For example, because of the levelling effect upon the value of a work point, raising the basic unit of account to the brigade level was expected to have an equalizing impact upon individual incomes of members belonging to different produc-tion teams. Therefore, cadres as well as individual members from

*New ideas and proposals, generally coming from the local
leadership or outside advisor, give rise to lengthy discussions among the home population before they are either
formalized and adopted, postponed or rejected.
(Discussion meeting in Tuyuan commune, Guangdong.)*

106

teams with a relatively high income tended to object to the proposed change because their income might decrease. A great deal
of argumentation was then needed to convince them that in the
longer run all the brigade, including themselves were likely to
benefit from the change. Quite often a long period of consultation appeared to be needed in order to bring about a reconcili-
ation between short-term and long-term interests. It seems that
in such campaigns of mass education the local Association of Poor
and Lower Middle Peasants or another mass organization generally
played a significant role. The role of these organizations, such
as the Youth League, the Women's Federation and the Association of
Poor and Middle Peasants, was most important during the first
decades after the revolution, as they acted as "transmission
belts" between the Communist Party and the rural masses. During
the first years of the Cultural Revolution, when the power of the
party and its inner cohesion were on the wane, the position of
these mass organizations was seriously affected. For example,
the Women's Federation, considered as too submissive to local
cadres, was dissolved.[1/] In 1972 it was revived, under a party
impregnated with the ideas of the Cultural Revolution. But after
1974, the mass organizations were again severely attacked by the
group that was later to be called the "Gang of Four". To quote
Michelle Loi on the Women's Federation, the Youth League and the
Federation of Trade Unions:

> "The Four accuse these associations of being 'dominated
> by the bourgeoisie'. Their leading cadres are accused of
> having 'forgotten the class struggle'. The Youth League has
> become a 'league of all the people', the trade unions
> 'unions of all the people' and the National Women's Feder-
> ation an organization working for 'class capitulation'."[2/]

Since Mao's death the mass organizations are attempting to
regain their function as "transmission belts", but no longer on a
class basis.

[1/] Michelle Loi, *op.cit.*, p.40.

[2/] *Ibid.*, p.52 (our translation).

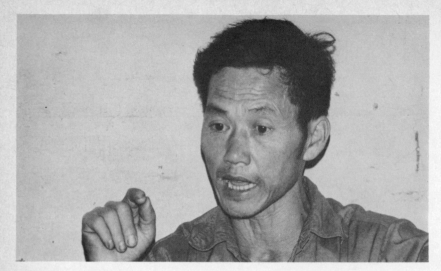

Images from discussion meetings in Tuyuan commune (Guangdong) and Longchi commune (Sichuan)

Another example of contradictions is the clash of interests between those in favour of reforestation of hillsides, and those who individually or as a production team possess sheep or cattle and are using the hillsides as grazing grounds. Only by assiduous education can the latter be convinced that they have to refrain from grazing there, as long as the planted trees are still young.

The important role of the local cadres in the decision-making process gives rise to the basic question of how the Cultural Revolution of 1966 and following years affected the procedures of direct democracy in rural areas. We had anticipated that a discussion of such problems, because of its relevance to issues that are still highly sensitive ideologically and psychologically, could meet with serious obstacles. However, whenever we raised the problem of popular participation in connection with more recent periods, we did not get the impression that we met with specific inhibitions. Our informants often even raised the problems they had encountered during the difficult period on their own accord. Discussing more recent periods even had advantages: while the memory of what exactly had happened in earlier periods (for example, during the Great Leap Forward) had grown somewhat vague, more recent developments were more clearly in mind and we were often able to obtain a detailed picture of them.

It is true that cadres at provincial or county level often provided us with a dark picture of the "ten lost years" that carried clear ideological overtones. But this over-simplified picture was usually corrected in conversation with local cadres and peasants when we asked for concrete information about *when* exactly a certain development or innovation had happened.

There was general agreement that the years 1967/1968, and sometimes also 1969, were a period of serious anarchic tendencies. It was a time during which cadres were often attacked by young activists using the slogans of the Cultural Revolution. Capable leaders were also attacked if their working style was considered

too authoritarian, as for example in the case of a prominent
leader in Liuji people's commune in Xinzhou county (Hubei province).   Wertheim came to know him in 1964 as an apparently very
competent manager but one who had a tendency to present his
commune as a kind of one-man show.   There was agreement among the
spokesmen of the different communes that in those years many
cadres were not able to provide effective leadership because
people would not listen to them.

But as of 1969 or 1970 in several places the picture
evidently changed.   The cadres, whether or not newly appointed,
had regained authority and several communes initiated construction
of infrastructural works, developed new collective enterprises or
took other initiatives.   It seemed plausible that the Cultural
Revolution, in spite of certain negative aspects, had released a
certain popular enthusiasm that could express itself in such
dynamic initiatives as the exploitation of coal mines (Longchi
commune), building new water works (Dongfeng commune), or extending the multi-cropping pattern (Liangjiafan commune).   But whenever we attempted to demonstrate to our escorts from the provincial
capital that, on the basis of the evidence presented by local
people, cadres as well as peasants, it would be wrong to view the
period of 1966-1976 as "a lost decade", they had their reply ready.
Innovations and achievements were never *owing to* but always *in
spite of* the Cultural Revolution, either because Zhou Enlai and
his associates had regained some power and issued directives to
pay full attention to production or because the peasantry were in-
telligent enough to ignore the directives of "Lin Biao and the
Gang of Four".   We retained serious doubts whether this preju-
diced way of arguing was in harmony with the new slogan of "seeking
truth from facts".   On the basis of our experiences we remain convinced that the Cultural Revolution was a period when peasants in
many places were motivated to develop all kinds of new and dynamic
initiatives.

It might not be so easy to obtain concrete evidence from the
people about the positive, educational aspects of the Cultural
Revolution at present, however.   People are afraid of being ident-

110

ified with supporters of the "Gang of Four" if they go against today's official line, which denies any positive aspects of the Cultural Revolution. But from the *factual* information we obtained about all kinds of important initiatives undertaken during that period we find it highly probable that popular participation in the countryside was a most significant aspect of what happened in those years, in spite of all kinds of anarchic excesses and painful experiences for many people and particularly cadres.

However, we also came across cases of anarchy erupting anew in the seventies. A striking example was Tuyuan commune (Guangdong province), where between 1971 and 1973 there had been three serious armed clashes between different brigades, all attributed to the nefarious influence of "Lin Biao and the Gang of Four". There had been fights between tens or even hundreds of peasants. As a result, production had been seriously affected. Whenever cadres wanted to mediate, it was they who were attacked; people would not listen to them. During 1974 and 1975 both cadres and peasants have "received education", in order to convince them that the peasantry has common interests, and that no deadly contradiction could exist among them; it was the "reactionary line" of Lin Biao that was at fault. As a consequence of the educational campaign both cadres and masses became aware of social reality, and an exchange of visits took place, in addition to "unity meetings". In this way, the problem was solved.

Certainly some other places we visited had also experienced troubled years. The case of Liangzhu commune (Zhejiang province), where there was a directive "not to produce for a wrong line" has already been mentioned. In another commune in the same province (Xihu) the quality of tea was said to have deteriorated for some years.

But, all in all, the total impression of what happened in the Chinese countryside did not seem to warrant at all an assessment of the whole period as "a lost decade". On the contrary, we formed the impression that great progress had been achieved

111

whenever the local leadership was able to stimulate the masses towards active and dynamic participation in local affairs. The example of Liangjiafan commune is a significant case in point.

On the other hand, whenever leaders who had come to the fore in the wake of the Cultural Revolution attempted to impose their ideas in an authoritarian and arbitrary way, serious dissensions were bound to arise and anarchic tendencies came to predominate.

While our historical approach, enquiring about modalities of popular participation regarding past policies, did provide us with important general information, we found that it was often difficult to receive precise information about such decision-making processes from the peasants, either because they actually did not remember or because they presented historical events in the light of their present ideological interpretation. However, we had also found that they had surprisingly few inhibitions about answering questions concerning present procedures; we attempted, therefore, to assess the role of popular participation in present rural strategies. Twice we were able to attend meetings in a commune that happened to take place during our stay.[1] Attending such local gatherings proved to be a very useful research tool in order to get an impression of the general atmosphere in connection with direct democracy at the base.

The first meeting was in Liangjiafan subcommune, where we were allowed to attend a gathering of production team leaders with the Revolutionary Committee to brigade No.1. Our hosts invited us to sit in chairs in front but we preferred to sit as unobtrusively as possible on a bench against the wall, and listen to (abridged) translations of what was being said. The chairman of the subcommune was also present, and in the beginning he tried to influence the discussion by making remarks; but since his presence at a regular meeting at brigade level was unusual, we asked him to

---

[1] A more detailed account of these two meetings is given in the appendix.

112

refrain from interfering, and he immediately complied.

*The Chairman of the Revolutionary Committee of Brigade No.1,
Liangjiafan subcommune (Hubei) opens a meeting of Production Team
Leaders by proposing the agenda for discussion.*

The problems discussed concerned matters of irrigation, of
rape-seed cultivation, and of seed selection for next year's rice
crop.   The brigade leader introduced and defined the problems to
be discussed, and solicited opinions from all those present.   He
did not actively participate in the debate by expressing his own
opinion (though the vice-chairman of the brigade, who also took
notes, did so).

We were most of all struck by the fact that all those
present participated in the discussion and appeared to be able to
express themselves quite freely (which confirmed our impression
that this was not a special show staged for us), and that nobody
seemed to dominate.   Stiefel found the type of direct democracy
we witnessed reminded him of citizens' gatherings in Swiss rural
communities.

At the end of the gathering (which lasted about one hour) the chairman defined a "consensus", and attempted to sum up and interpret the debates and to formulate conclusions for practical implementation of the measures agreed.

An interesting moment came at the end of the meeting when Mr. Peng Sihan, member of the Revolutionary Committee of Baiguo commune, who had attended the last part of the discussion, expressed open criticism of the work of one specific team, with which he was particularly concerned because he conducted certain experiments on their field.

Another gathering we attended was a small meeting of cadres (work group leaders and a few members with administrative tasks) of one specific production team in Longchi commune. The problems to be discussed were: the appointment of candidates for the people's congress of Emei county, and planning for the winter wheat crop. Emei county is one of 66 administrative units selected from all over China where, for the first time and on an experimental basis, the people could elect in the second half of 1979 their representatives up to the county level. The chairman started by giving a general exposition. Fourteen delegates were to be elected from Longchi commune and ten among them should be members of the Communist Party (in order to ensure "direction by the Party"); cadres were also to be represented. The delegates would also have to represent different sectors of rural life such as industry, agriculture, education and culture and health care. More than fourteen candidates could be nominated as the commune would arrange a pre-election.

One old man, a party member who always attended gatherings and expressed himself more than others did in ideological terms, proposed a cadre from the commune who "unites with the masses and applies the mass line well". Another speaker proposed the vice-chairman of the Revolutionary Committee of the commune (a comparatively aged man, who during our discussions with the commune leadership most of the time kept silent), saying: "Since he has come to work here, he has always remained honest". We had an

Meeting of cadres of Production Team No.3,
Taoyuan Brigade, Longchi Commune (Sichuan) to
select candidates for the elections to the
people's congress at the county level and to
discuss problems of winter wheat planting.

An elderly peasant makes a point at the meeting
in Taoyuan Brigade.

inkling that this was a way of expressing veiled criticism of other leaders. There were also some speakers who proposed female delegates (although our interpreter was the only woman present). As in Liangjiafan, the chairman did not interfere in the discussion; this time it was he who kept notes.

During the discussion on winter wheat the serious problem of drainage was raised. Ditches had to be deepened; this would also help to prevent dispersal and waste of fertilizer.

One of the speakers said: "We, cadres, have to provide good leadership - we are 'the brains' of the masses; the quality of work depends on us".

During the gathering one of the speakers raised the idea of experimenting with a mixture of two kinds of oil (one extracted from coal, which is abundant in the region) as a cheap kind of insecticide, mainly against the rice-stem-borer - an idea that provoked a lively discussion in which a district cadre, who accompanied us, participated.[1]

After the meeting closed, we inquired what was going to happen with the list of prospective candidates. It appeared that *after* the meeting of cadres a plenary session of all the production team members would be held, in which names for nomination of candidates would be proposed. The production team would send the proposal to the brigade, which would forward all the lists received from the production teams to the commune. The commune would then publish all the names submitted - over one hundred. Then the list would again be referred to the brigades for discussion within each production team and at brigade level the list would be abridged to 28 candidates (double the number of the seats to be filled). Half of these would finally be elected.

---

[1] According to Professor J. de Wilde, entomologist at the School of Agriculture in Wageningen, a use of oil mixtures as an insecticide for an annual crop is not a good idea in view of the danger of combustion of the plants.

116

Other ideas raised at the meeting, which had a preliminary character, would be discussed with the masses; afterwards, formal decisions would be taken. We inquired why two of the eight present at the meeting had remained silent all the time, even on questions of agriculture. The reply was that they were cadres with administrative tasks (one of them was the bookkeeper charged with noting which workers were present in view of calculating work points, the other was a guard of the granary) and consequently they did not consider themselves experts in cultivation methods.

Again, our impression was that the element of basic democracy, evidenced by the way the meeting was conducted, might be of greater significance as an element of "popular participation" than the *formal* aspects of the election of candidates for the county congress.

To sum up, it emerged from our general investigations about present decision-making processes at the local level that the mass line is still very much operative in actual practice. What we witnessed during the two meetings was actually a practical implementation of the mass line concept. Marc Blecher had called this in an article "the mass line as a *consensual* theory of local politics".[1]

The key point of what we saw is indeed that decisions are taken by consensus: as a first step *clear policy goals* are formulated by cadres of the party at higher levels (central, provincial, county); the concrete forms that they should take in particular situations is not clearly spelled out. At the local level the issue is taken up by the local cadres - the issue is thus almost always put on the agenda by the authorities (usually at commune level) - and through the mass organizations it is filtered down to the population. A sometimes long period of mainly informal discussion, education and persuasion (during which the mass organiz-

---

[1] See Marc Blecher, "Consensual Politics in Rural Chinese Communities", *Modern China*, Vol.5, No.1, January 1979.

ations ensure a perpetual two-way flow of ideas and opinions between the cadres and the masses) ensues. This reflects the basic "mass line idea" that the *translation of policy into action* must involve the opinions of the masses, based on their knowledge of actual conditions. Once a consensus seems to emerge, and a decision can be taken, this decision is often first taken on an *experimental* basis. This again reflects adherence to a basic "mass line idea": the *testing* of new policies reflects the political recognition that the masses' reactions are vital to the policy's success and also that the cadres can never predict these reactions fully in advance.

It appears that while the *Party*, and its cadres at the local level, indisputably control a *de facto power monopoly*, it is tempered by the fact that they *must* take into account the masses' opinion. For political reasons they cannot go for a long time *against* the masses.

An interesting question is whether new developments in China will undermine the future functioning of this type of direct democracy at the base. There are two factors in the campaign for the "four modernizations" that in the long run might affect the element of popular participation in rural strategies as a form of direct democracy:

1. Increase in scale in the wake of modernization and mechanization, with fewer employment opportunities for certain groups;
2. The factor of haste involved in meeting precise targets within a given period.

In the research proposal that formed the basis for the present exploratory mission, these factors were discussed as follows:

> "Active people's participation is evidently much easier to achieve in small units. In a context of traditional agriculture, procedures of direct democracy can be pursued on a local level, among people who know each other well. This becomes more and more difficult when economic development is pursued in larger units; it seems well-nigh

impossible on higher levels of decision-making, as soon as distances have become greater, personal acquaintance with persons has become less, and the issues at stake have become more complicated. The introduction, in our Western society, of formal democracy by delegation has been a consequence of a modernization process requiring ever greater units of economic action. It could be argued that, although direct democracy might be feasible within a peasant society characterized by small units, modernization will inevitably lead to more authoritarian ways of decision-making and problem-solving."1/

Our mission did not provide specific data that could serve to illustrate a trend as described in the above quotation. New situations resulting from a raising of the level of the basic unit of account could lead, of course, in principle to a more managerial working style and to a decrease in direct democratic consultations at the base. But since either the original production teams are being preserved as nuclear units, or more specialized work groups are being formed, such a decrease in popular participation through increase in size will be difficult to demonstrate except by more intensive research methods than were available to us.

The potentially negative effect on popular participation inherent in a strategy operating with strict targets and time-tables was striking. If the period of the Cultural Revolution could be assessed as one where long-term planning was regrettably lacking, the present leadership seems overly concerned with fixed timetables. Even though the strongly exaggerated expectations about "great leaps forward" in production, which dominated the atmosphere in China during the late seventies, seem to have been cut down now to more modest proportions, the way of thinking in terms of fixed targets for 1985, for 1990, for 2000 or even beyond is still very much in evidence. Actual achievement of these targets requires speed and, generally speaking, extensive consultation of the people is difficult to reconcile with speed. (We

---

1/ *Democratic Centralism and the Mass Line in Rural China - an assessment of the Chinese experience in popular participation*, UNRISD/79/C.24, June 1979, pp.7/8.

119

can recall Mao Zedong's and Zhou Enlai's warning against rashness and their pleas for "great perseverance and patience" in attempting to persuade the people of the desirability of a proposed policy.) In an atmosphere where both at the central and at the regional and local levels rural strategies are becoming target-oriented, the demand for a tenacious and patient campaign of persuasion may easily be sacrificed in order to be able to show quick results.

It is particularly in connection with present family planning policies that we were struck by the dangerous aspects of setting fixed targets. We pointed out earlier certain weaknesses of the present population policies as such, particularly in regions where farm mechanization is difficult to achieve. In this context it is primarily the aspect of compulsion backed by stern economic penalties that run counter to the old Maoist principle of patient education and persuasion.

During our mission, we did not encounter signs of discontent among the people over the harsh restrictions on child-bearing, but we hardly had time to do so; moreover, there were no women in the research team that went inland.

However, in the *People's Daily* of September 2, 1980, in an article dealing with family planning in rural areas, the author refers to:

"...various practical problems which give rise to misgivings among the masses about having only one child. For example, they worry about who will take care of them in their old age, and about health care for the only child... These problems affect the immediate interests of the masses";

and, further on:

"In an attempt to limit China's population to 1,200 million by the end of this century, the State Council has issued a call to all people in the country advocating one-child families. This is an important measure which affects the *speed* (our italics) and future of the four modernizations."

The aim of the policy is described as "to remedy the country's poverty and backwardness *in a short time*" (our italics).

There is obviously a basic contradiction between this accent on speed and the recent slogan "haste makes waste".

The family planning strategy is an extreme instance of targets and timetables being imposed from above without any proper consultation of the people concerned. As far as production targets are concerned, there is a longstanding habit of consulting collective units and their members, as part and parcel of annual planning procedures. Tentative plans are being sent from the centre down along the hierarchical line to the production team for discussion, and then up again to the brigade, commune, county, administrative region, province and centre. This up-and-down flow allows for a crucial balancing of the interests of the state and wider collective unit (commune, brigade) with those of the team and the individual. Moreover, there are consultations between the different levels throughout the plan period, and frequent adjustments are made. The collective units have thus always enjoyed a right to object, with varying success, against excessive demands made on their productive capacity. However, even then a fixing of long-term goals as quantitative targets to be achieved in the process of the "four modernizations" does not leave much room for popular consultation.

But we have to make an important distinction between participation at the level of local collective units and participation among their members. As we have seen earlier, the formation of people's communes has created a considerable amount of decentralization in the decision-making process in rural life and the Cultural Revolution, which initially led to a weakening of the central party leadership, has in practice even strengthened local self-government.

The tightening of party discipline since Mao's death, expressed in the renewed formulation of the Leninist concept of "democratic centralism", is likely to lead to a stricter supervision of local party organs by the central party leadership. Since at the local level management of the collective units is, as we could observe, still under strong influence of local party committees (the recent separation of party and government at the central level has not yet spread to local government), one could expect a tendency towards stricter observance of central party directives.

It was therefore surprising to us to observe the extent to which the people's communes we visited disposed of a freedom to interpret and adapt these directives to local conditions; raising the basic unit of account and assistance to poor teams, already cited, are two examples. As far as the implementation of directives on family planning is concerned, we were told that the rigidity and strictness observed by the leadership of Longchi commune was far from general even within Emei county.

One could easily take this flexibility as an expression of a measure of popular participation. However, a different interpretation was given to us by a number of Chinese we met: a reluctance among provincial, prefecture or county level authorities to commit themselves too strongly to a certain political or ideological line, for fear of the top party leadership replacing it with a new one. Such shirking of responsibility by the government bureaucracy at the intermediate level in present-day China was mentioned to us more than once. As a result it is the local leadership that is compelled to actually take many rural policy decisions, and to translate general guidelines into concrete actions.

However, it would be wrong to assume that this amount of local self-government automatically means increased participation by the *individual* peasants. We were warned by a good China expert living in Hong Kong, who is generally in sympathy with Chinese policies, that authority at the local level may be as authoritarian as dictatorship at the top. There are still many feudal remnants in rural China that account for a tendency to submit to local tyrants without question.[1]   Therefore, we must distinguish between participation in decision-making by the people and participation through self-government by local authorities. Our impression was that there are places where local leaders, particularly if they are of local peasant origin, do really represent the wishes of the rural masses.   On the other hand, leaders appointed from the outside may be more inclined to apply central directives rigidly or even to overdo their compliance in order to satisfy their superiors.

Therefore it would seem dangerous, as was announced in the Chinese press[2], that peasant leaders who may lack certain educational qualifications would be replaced by leaders with "higher qualifications" who are mainly of urban origin.   Selecting local leadership on the basis of formal diplomas could certainly endanger relationships between cadres and masses, and jeopardize the principle of popular participation at the local level.

Generally speaking, we can say that the Chinese Revolution of 1949, the following revolutionary changes and the institutionalization of people's communes have set the *objective preconditions* for real popular participation and democracy at the local level. Whether there is democracy in actual fact, and to what extent, depends on the quality of local leadership and the political cohesion and consciousness of the local community.

----

[1] Jack Gray rightly pointed out in a comment to an earlier draft of this study, that throughout Chinese history "when centralized bureaucracy is relaxed on the grounds that it is divorced from local conditions and tends to stifle local initiative or that it is dictatorial, there has always been a tendency for the central élite to be replaced by a local élite, and the cure has often proved worse than the disease".   According to Gray this explains much of the excesses of the Cultural Revolution.

[2] See *Beijing Review*, 11/8/1980, No.32, p.7.

There is one more problem to mention in connection with the issue of popular participation and the mass line. As we have seen, in earlier periods a good deal of mass education and mass mobilization was performed through the local Poor and Lower Middle Peasants Associations. The new policies that remove the specific prerogatives of poorer peasants and their offspring are resulting, as we were able to observe, in a gradual extinction or even a formal abolition of these associations. It is still too early to say whether the new "Peasants' Associations", created in several places in accordance with the new conceptions about "class (that is to say, without discrimination against landlords or rich farmers and their progeny), could replace the old associations as organizational forms for mass education, mobilization and participation.[1]

In some places that we visited, the local Revolutionary Committees were being replaced by Management Committees of the kind abolished in the sixties during the Cultural Revolution. In other places, such a change had not yet occurred. But we did not have the impression that the change was more than one of terminology. Though it was evidently the intention to do away with revolutionary committees eventually (as has happened already in the higher reaches of government administration) we did not feel that this would lead to any fundamental changes, except for increased stress on hierarchy and discipline.

Our general conclusion is that, despite increased stress on principles of *formal* democracy and on procedures intended to strengthen the rule of law, recent changes connected with promoting "the four modernizations" are more likely to decrease the influence of direct democracy at the basis. Popular participation, which was at the root of the successes of Maoist strategy for three decades, seems to be threatened now by processes that will

---

[1] See, for example, a report from the Hubei provincial radio service of 13 January 1981 on the reorganization of the poor and lower-middle peasants' associations into peasant associations as a result of "the changed class situation in the rural areas". *SWB*, FE/6624/BII/2, 16.1.81.

make it more and more difficult to maintain intact the specific
distinguishing features of the Chinese development model.

——————— oOo ———————

GENERAL CONCLUSIONS

The duration of our exploratory mission was too short and the range of territories visited too limited to warrant anything like definitive conclusions regarding past and present developments in China as a whole. However, some provisional conclusions may be drawn, on the basis of the scattered experiences described above, supplemented with data collected during earlier visits and a study of the available literature.

A preliminary word of caution: any visitor to China brings, consciously or not, a set of preconceived images and ideas about Chinese development and the ideological and political currents that seem dominant at the time of his visit. The myth of China as one homogeneous unit pushed ahead along one set of clear policies defined by central authorities in Beijing is certainly the first to crumble if one visits places such as those on our tour. Again and again we were struck by the tremendous diversity of local situations, not only topographically and climatically but in terms of sometimes quite radically different interpretations of central policy guidelines and of the historical experiences of local communities. A large number of political and ideological currents and experiences seem, at all levels and at any time, to be in continuous dialectical confrontation in China. This makes Chinese reality extremely complex; all efforts by foreign visitors and commentators to grasp Chinese reality in terms of clear categories and black-and-white images are bound to fail.

Nevertheless, in spite of the internal diversity, Chinese social reality presents enough inner cohesion and convergence to allow an assessment of achievements and problems of the Chinese people in more general terms. The possibility for both of us to make comparisons with developments in several parts of South and Southeast Asia, on the basis of personal acquaintance with the situation in those countries, has provided us with a general background knowledge enabling us to assess the real significance of

127

achievements in China since the establishment of the People's
Republic.

1.   There can be no doubt that the Chinese achievements, both in
the realm of agricultural production and in the field of distribution[1/], are impressive if compared with any large agrarian
country in South and Southeast Asia.   On the one hand, with its
enormous size and population China is still an "underdeveloped"
country, economically belonging to the Third World.   If the level
of welfare is compared with that of Western Europe or North
America, it is still very poor and backward.   But in three decades
it has laid a basis for further sound development, in contrast
with the progressive "development of underdevelopment"[2/] typical
of many Third World countries.

     As we have pointed out, anything like egalitarianism has
never been on the Chinese programme.   But some of the most important sources of inequality, for example, exploitative landlordism, have been eliminated;   and there has been steady attention to
the basic needs of the rural population.   Guaranteeing a minimal
subsistence level for everyone has been one of the greatest
achievements of Chinese rural strategy.   Its significance can be
realized better if one takes account of a distinction made in Java
(Indonesia).   There, rural economists[3/] make a distinction between
two categories of people: the *berkecukupans* and the *kekurangans*.
The former are those who have enough: they *know* that tomorrow
they will eat.   The *kekurangans* are those who live from day to
day, not knowing what tomorrow will bring: they have *too little*.
The second category, those living below the poverty line, are

---

[1/] As far as distribution is concerned, this has been convincingly
demonstrated by Keith Griffin and Ashwani Saith in *The Pattern
of Income Inequality in Rural China*, Bangkok, 1980.

[2/] An expression coined by André Gunder Frank.

[3/] D.H. Penny and Masri Singarimbun, *Population and Poverty in
Rural Java: Some Economic Arithmetic from Sriharjo*, 1973.

estimated by an outstanding Indonesian rural sociologist to in-
clude about half the rural population of Java.[1]

It seems that in China, basically everyone knows that tomorrow he will eat. Here is maybe the greatest achievement of
the Chinese rural strategy. And it is this basic security of
livelihood that makes regular participation of the masses in
political and economic decision-making at all possible. In other
countries of Asia, where a majority of the rural population live
at subsistence level and in a continual state of insecurity, participation in everyday politics appears as a luxury that only few
can afford. Popular participation then takes at most the form of
some formal procedures, such as elections, or of a violent and
desperate outburst against social inequalities and injustices.

2.   At present the Cultural Revolution and the period of domination by "the Gang of Four" are presented by both the Chinese
leadership and the Chinese press as a disastrous period ("the lost
decade"). Some leaders even extend the catastrophic developments
to the period starting with the Great Leap Forward, such as Deng
Xiaoping in his lecture of January 16, 1980.

One of our main conclusions was that, whatever consequences
the Cultural Revolution and its aftermath might have had for
industrial production, for science and higher education, the
balance sheet for rural areas was distinctly more ambiguous.

---

[1] See, for example, Sajogyo, "The Poverty Line and Minimum Food
Needs", *Kompas*, 18/11/1977. See also W.F. Wertheim, "Aid to
the Poor - or Betting on the Poor?", in *Development of
Societies: The Next Twenty-Five Years*, Proceedings of ISS 25th
Anniversary Conference, The Hague, 1979, pp.86 ff.

President Suharto of Indonesia confirmed, in October 1980, that
in Java "some 40 million Indonesians or 50 percent of the total
population are still living below the poverty line". However,
he boasts that this is an "achievement of our goals", because
allegedly "in 1969, 90 percent of the Indonesians were still
living below the poverty line" (*Antara News Bulletin*, The Hague,
21/10/80). This claim has no foundation whatsoever.

Although in some places we encountered negative effects of excesses committed during those ten years, many excellent initiatives (e.g. infrastructural works and diversification of production, which are at present paying off by appreciably increased productive capacity) were undertaken either during the Great Leap Forward or during the allegedly "lost" decade. It was precisely the national movement of emulation brought about by the Cultural Revolution that allowed first for the completion of basic land-and-water schemes in the Chinese countryside and, second, for the many initiatives taken to diversify the rural economy by promoting local industry, collective animal husbandry and other sidelines of production. The present economic successes seem to be largely possible thanks to this infrastructural work undertaken during the Cultural Revolution.

We also strongly doubt the wisdom of the present campaign denouncing the Cultural Revolution. Presenting a period during which many elements of the Maoist strategy were still operative as one of pure disaster seems to cause disenchantment and loss of faith in the Communist Party, particularly among the younger people who have not known pre-revolutionary China. They may easily argue that if the party was capable of making mistakes of such magnitude that they brought economic development to a standstill, there is no guarantee that it is now on the right track. Completely denouncing past achievements might also lead to a loss of faith in socialism as an economic system. The cynicism of the younger generation towards official policy and institutions clearly preoccupies the present Chinese leaders. In several discussions in Beijing, both in 1979 and in 1980, this was cited by higher cadres as one of the main problems that China is facing today.

3. At present, it is mainly the backwardness of China in comparison with the industrialized world that is being stressed by higher authorities in China. This is attributed partly to lack of contact, particularly since the Cultural Revolution, with Western and Japanese scientists and hence also with the rapid progress of foreign technology. But the Chinese were also unaware of

130

what was happening in many Third World countries, particularly in
those such as India, Bangladesh and Indonesia, that in some
respects can be compared with China.   Lack of pride in their own
considerable achievements is due partly to lack of acquaintance
with what that same foreign technology has wrought in the Third
World, and at what social cost.

The present trend in China to swallow advanced foreign technology lock, stock and barrel indicates that the Chinese are still
insufficiently aware of the relationship between technology and
the economic and social environment where it is introduced.   There
are positive lessons to be learnt from the advanced industrial
world but also, equally important, negative lessons from the backward underdeveloped countries.[1/]   "Finding truth from facts" also
would imply learning more about the dangers of foreign technology
as applied in neighbouring Asian countries. At times it seems that
some of the Chinese leaders wrongly assume that because of its
"socialist system" China would automatically be immune to such
dangers.

4.   A regular visitor to China over the past decades is struck
by the drastic changes of direction that occur periodically.
Denouncing an earlier period and eulogizing the present belonged
to the accepted style of propaganda.   Whereas during the Cultural
Revolution the period when Liu Shaoqi was in charge was denounced
and a line drawn between developments *before* and *after* the
Cultural Revolution (*dageming qian* and *dageming hou*);   a similar
line is now drawn between the period dominated by "Lin Biao and
the Gang of Four" and the era of "the Four Modernizations".

One could therefore ask whether the recurrent curves in
China's development belong to a deliberate strategy of the Communist Party.   There is some reason to ask, because the image of a

---

[1/] On 18 October 1979, Wertheim gave a lecture in Beijing, organized by the Friendship Association, on "Negative Lessons from
the Third World".

Advanced technology coexists today in China in all fields with traditional technology. But even a "socialist system" may not be immune to the negative social consequences of too hasty an introduction of advanced foreign technology.

spiral-like development has been repeatedly used by Mao Zedong. For example, in Point Two of the 16 Points issued by the Central Committee on 8 August 1966, during the early phase of the Cultural Revolution, a distinction was made between the general (strategic) line of the party, and the oft-repeated tactical zig-zags. In the Maoist interpretation of socialist development dialectical fluctuations played an important role. To understand this, we have to realize that the Chinese strategy of development seems to be inherently different from what Westerners imagine such a strategy to be. The Chinese strategy is *not* necessarily as most Western strategies are supposed to be; it is *per se* contradictory oscillating, combining seemingly irreconcilable opposites in a dialectical unity.

A dialectical way of thinking, in terms of a unity of seemingly contrasting elements, is in accordance with Chinese philosophical thinking.[1]

However, it is highly questionable whether the present leadership would still be prepared to view the march towards "the Four Modernizations" as a zig-zag one. The way they are setting fixed targets and strict timetables for long-term developments rather points towards a linear view of development borrowed from Western models.

---

[1] See also Johan Galtung's paper: *Is there a Chinese Strategy of Development*, University Sains Malaysia, Penang, (mimeo). In a comment on an earlier draft of this study, Marshall Wolfe has conceptualized these policy swings in terms of a series of successive "shock waves" and has explained them as an inevitable outcome of the determination of the central Chinese leadership to transform rural society rapidly and uniformly in spite of the diversity and inertia of this society and the relative weakness of transmission belts. According to Wolfe, policy thus has taken the form of "a series of shock waves, expressed in simple slogans, travelling from the centre to the periphery, intended to change ways of thinking as much as economic and social practices, becoming distorted and exaggerated in transmission, interacting in unpredictable ways with local problems and sources of conflict, the repercussions gradually travelling back to the centre, giving rise to central attempts to rectify the distortions by exaggerated emphasis on their contraries, and eventually by new shock waves."

In our view, despite all kinds of seemingly radical turn-abouts in China, there has been a basic long-term *continuity* of policy as actually pursued in the Chinese countryside between 1949 and 1980. There is much more *continuity and coherence* in a long-term socialist transformation than the present leaders want to admit. The zig-zag line of development corresponds to an alternation of periods of mass mobilization with periods of calm. Both are together necessary and positive as a whole in the long run.

The possibility cannot be excluded that, after the present exceedingly strong deflection of the pointer towards "stability" and "growth", internal conditions and inevitable disappointments will again produce a new backlash and lead to what is sometimes called the "Yenan way".[1] We do not see this as very likely in the foreseeable future, if only because social revolutions ending in a kind of Thermidor seldom show a return to a more radical line. But as the Chinese pattern of development has repeatedly deviated from earlier revolutionary models, a new swing to the left remains within the realm of possibility, the more so since the Chinese way of attacking problems has thus far shown a basic wisdom, and has never suffered extreme solutions for long periods. "Seeking truth from facts" also implies turning back on one's steps (or on "great leaps forward") as soon as these are proved to have been in a wrong direction.

One of our local hosts in Wuhan described the Chinese Revolution as follows: "It is like the Yangtse river: it flows east, with many turnabouts and meanders, but in the final analysis it flows east, steadily, in spite of countercurrents."

5. Finally, we would like to draw some general conclusions about popular participation.

---

[1] See for example Mark Selden, *The Yenan Way in Revolutionary China*, 1971.

Generally speaking, developments in China appear to confirm the view that successes in both production and distribution depend on the rate of true popular participation. This participation was at the root of the successes in development achieved by the Chinese during the fifties and early sixties, in spite of the serious reverses during the three catastrophic years following the Great Leap Forward. Contrary to the experience of so many Third World countries, the Chinese peasantry was motivated to join forces to overcome all kinds of economic handicaps and natural impediments as land reform was carried out and followed by gradual collectivization of agriculture and other rural activities. Successful appeals to the peasantry to prevent flooding by reinforcing dams and dykes, to fight droughts by fetching water from ponds and rivers, or to build terraces on hill slopes, were possible by the existence of people's communes. In 1964, in Liuji commune (in Hubei province) Wertheim witnessed a collective anti-drought campaign in action, during which no able-bodied worker, male or female, was to be found at home: all were at work watering the fields to save the cotton crop. Similarly, even during the years of bad harvests (1959-1961) a fair distribution system motivated the peasants to carry on, despite serious hardships experienced by everyone.

The evidence available to us about rural developments during the decade 1966-1976 again confirms that this development was dynamic and positive in regions and during periods when local leaders succeeded in arousing enthusiasm and active participation among the peasant masses. On the other hand, whenever the Cultural Revolution and its aftermath created a great distance between leaders and masses, or led to anarchic situations in which the cadres were unable to assert their authority, development would occasionally come to a standstill.

Similarly, the present line of "four modernizations" will succeed whenever local leadership acts in conformity with the wishes and basic interests of the broad masses. If, on the other hand, the management style is authoritarian and promotes lopsided investment and unequal distribution, then in spite of a momentary increase in overall production and profits, it will in the long run prove difficult to mobilize people in pursuit of aims they do not perceive as being in harmony with their best interests. Too great a stress on numerical targets may estrange the mass of the people from their leaders. Even when initiatives are increasingly taken from above, as they will be in the future as a result of modernization and mechanization and the ensuing increase in size of relevant economic units, active participation of the people remains a precondition for effective government.

According to the present leadership's views, popular participation should be ensured by the introduction of laws and of democratic forms. However, bearing in mind experiences in Western countries, it is doubtful that formal institutions and laws of representative democracy are a sufficient guarantee of real participation. Maybe the creation of extensive legal provisions was indispensable in the present development phase of China; this aspect was certainly neglected in the past. But *without* elements of basic informal democracy by consultation at the base, strategies based on the implementation of laws will not work properly. In the past, observance of the "mass line" was a significant factor in achieving all kinds of successes in China. The "mass line", is still cited as a basic policy principle[1]; it would be regrettable if lip service continued to be paid to it but, in fact it were all but relinquished in favour of a democracy exclusively based on the Western principle of delegation and representation.

---

[1] In his speech of 7 September 1980, referred to earlier, Hua Guofeng mentioned consulting "workers and peasants" in the process of "mapping out our long-term programme" only in passing. The paragraph read under the heading "The mass line is the essential way to map out our long-term programme" for the rest only pays attention to involving "large numbers of experts" in the discussion (*Beijing Review*, 22/9/1980, No.38). Is this what the present leadership in China understands by the term "mass line"?

However, the extent to which informal democratic procedures at the base can be preserved in a process of modernization and increase in size remains to be seen. In order to acquire a deeper insight into such relationships further research, specifically focused upon definite aspects of this general problem will be necessary. Our exploratory mission has led us to the conclusion that, under the present conditions in China, such more specific research in the field, preferably with the *active* participation of Chinese social researchers, is feasible if co-operation on the part of the Chinese authorities can be obtained.

——————— oOo ———————

APPENDIX I

Account of Local Level Meetings Attended by Wertheim and Stiefel and their Interpreter, Mrs. Wang Huiying

A. <u>Meeting on 8 October 1979 of the Production Team Leaders with the Revolutionary Committee of Brigade No.1 of Liangjiafan Sub-Commune (Baiguo Commune, Macheng District, Hubei Province)</u>

Instead of seating ourselves in rattan armchairs at the front of the meeting room as proposed by our hosts, we prefer to sit as unobtrusively as possible on a bench against the wall. There are 24 participants, including one woman in charge of female work within the brigade.

The meeting starts with a lengthy introduction by the brigade Chairman.   The following items are in the agenda:

1. What kind of measures to take against the prolonged drought;
2. A plan for the selection of rape-seed varieties to be sown after the late rice harvest;
3. Selection of the late rice varieties to be sown in 1980, on the basis of results obtained so far.

The brigade Chief solicits opinions from all those present.

The Chairman of the subcommune, Mr. Cheng Yundong, who is also present (evidently in view of our attendance at the meeting) immediately takes the floor.   He thinks that, as far as rice seed selection is concerned, one could try to make a comparison between two different strains; he proposes that the comparison be undertaken in a planned and systematic way.   Then the leaders of production teams take the floor one after the other.

139

An elderly peasant, leader of Team No.8 is in favour of one specific rice variety, which is better suited for large areas. He is against experimenting with two different strains, sown on the same type of land, and prefers a strain that was already successful in one special field.

The leader of Team No.11 admits that their harvest was not very good; the seeds were mediocre. This time selection should be done diligently. He would prefer to experiment with three different varieties, each to be sown on one third of the fields. He explains the measures his team proposes to take.

The leader of Team No.2 observes that all the speakers are only discussing the plans of their own teams. He would prefer to discuss the problem more in general. His idea is that it would be preferable to experiment with different strains, in different proportions (not all of them on an equal footing), taking account of past experiences, which seem to indicate that some strains promise greater success than others.

The Production Team leader of Team No.10, recalling that his area belongs to the "high and stable yield" fields, says he would prefer to select only two varieties for his team.

The discussion turns to the selection of rape-seed; Team No. 10 is ready to sow.

The Vice-Chairman of the brigade, who keeps the notes, and speaks in a rather loud tone, discusses criteria for selection of the different varieties. The main point is that they should be resistant to frost. Lessons from the past must be taken into account. Last year some of the varieties selected had proved not to be the best ones.

The leader of Team No.7 agrees with the Vice-Chairman and argues that the rape-seed varieties that proved to be less resistant to frost have to be rejected.

He also recounts the experiences of his Team and mentions the percentages of land sown with each variety of rice. He is in favour of making comparisons between *three* different strains.

The brigade Chairman hardly intervenes in the discussion. The President of the subcommune sometimes intervenes but since his presence does not conform to usual practice, Mrs. Wang (at Stiefel's request) asks him not to interfere so as to make the meeting as normal as possible.

The leader of Team No.3, an elderly peasant with a lot of experience, explains that his Team had a nursery for rape-seed, but results from it were not conclusive; at present they were taking additional precautions, in order to attain full security.

The Vice-Chairman then argues that measures are needed against drought. There is shortage of water. Precautions must be taken at an earlier stage. Each Team should rapidly take action.

The leader of Team No.16 urges that the pumps used in the hills should be sent immediately to the irrigated area (at present the pumps are inside the brigade territory).

The leader of Team No.9 asks for information on the surface area used for nursing rape-seed. The answer is: nine *mou*. He would also like to use *two* varieties for the late rice crop, in a proportion of 60 and 40 percent. At present the women are picking cotton, whereas men are doing the pumping in the hills.

The elderly leader of Team No.15 reports that they have kept last year's seeds; but the rape-seed was of a bad quality. They will not use this variety any more.

The leader of the female Team says: the anti-drought campaign will not create problems for the cotton harvest if the pumps situated in the hills are used, but problems may arise for the rape-seed cultivation in the hilly area. Measures will have to be taken to safeguard the rape-seed crop.

The leader of Team No.1 calls for immediate precautions against drought as the brigade is not well prepared to face it. As for rice cultivation, he is in favour of choosing two varieties.

The leader of Team No.4 reports that they have at present no problems yet with drought; but there is not enough water in the pond. He recommends taking water from the commune's big water tank, for all eventualities (everyone laughs).

As for rape-seed cultivation, he proposes that special tasks be assigned to each person, and that work points be calculated according to the way each task is fulfilled.

The Vice-Chairman intervenes to say that in transplanting rape-seed the tasks will have to be equally distributed.

As the discussion starts to become a bit heated the leader of Team No.4 says: "Some people say that this or that variety is good; however, before deciding we have to test first. We should never use varieties on a large scale without prior testing." He adds that rape-seed sprouts should be protected against chickens and that this should be assigned as a special task.

The leader of Team No.6 reports that his team has been successful in fighting pests; they had no problems with rape-seed either. Most of the men are at present fighting the drought, or fetching fertilizer, while most of the women are picking cotton. There is, however, a shortage of labour.

The Vice-Chairman observes that it would be a good idea to·make individual team members responsible for a special field planted with rape-seed; these members should also guard the sprouts against chickens. He will control the work; if there is any damage somewhere, the team will be held responsible.

Throughout the discussion the Chairman of the brigade has hardly ever taken the floor. He has let a sometimes heated discussion develop, in which all those present have had a chance to freely express their opinions. He now rises, sums up the discussion, defines a consensus and announces the decisions that have emerged from the meeting, demanding that all the team leaders unify methods within the brigade as far as possible:

1. Selection of seeds: the proportion should be 30%, 60% and 10% of the three varieties discussed.
2. The struggle against drought: in some teams the situation is better, in others it is worse. Those who are not ready with their measures have to catch up quickly. Each team is entitled to withdraw water from the big water tank. In the next two days all fields that need irrigation have to be irrigated.
3. Good management of rape-seed is very important. Responsibility for each field will be allocated to individual members, and work points calculated accordingly. Next year's crop of rape-seed should exceed 100,000 *jin*.
4. Great care must be taken now to fight against insects that can harm the crops.
5. All teams must take advantage of the good weather to bring in the rest of the cotton harvest.

Mr. Peng Sihan, Vice-Chairman of Baiguo commune, who has attended the latter part of the discussion, agrees with the brigade leader's points, and makes some further remarks. The main one is that each person should feel responsible for the piece of land allotted to him. In addition the struggle against pests must receive attention.

"On return to your teams you should make haste!" Peng adds that "the meeting has taken the whole afternoon. Talking is one thing; but now action is needed. It was a good meeting; but the conclusions now have to be put into practice." If the anti-drought action is not successful, there will be uncertainty about next year's crop.

He adds that half a *mou* should be enough for each person to take care of. Quality of work was as important as the quantity.

The Chairman of Baiguo commune, Mr. Zhou Guomin, who has also meanwhile come in, makes some remarks about Team No. 1; it is the team whose land includes an experimental field, under the supervision of Mr. Peng Sihan, the Vice-Chairman. It is generally assumed that Team No. 1 is excellent; but he thinks Team No. 8 is at least as good.

A representative from Macheng district who has accompanied us on our visit to Baiguo and is in charge of external relations of the district, also makes a few remarks, implying that only the experimental field of Team No. 1 is really good, not the rest.

Mr. Peng adds that Team No. 1 is only performing the initial selection work; it had taken good care of the experimental fields but had neglected other fields. "Other teams have already surpassed you as far as results in general are concerned!" Some teams, he points out, have to pay more attention to selection.

The meeting ends with Wertheim expressing thanks on behalf of Stiefel and himself for the opportunity to attend the meeting.

B. Meeting on 13 October 1979, of Cadres belonging to Team No. 3 Taoyuan Brigade, Longchi Commune, Emei District, Sichuan Province

The meeting takes place in a granary, where bundles of maize ears are hanging from the ceiling, and bags of straw are being kept. The granary is situated on the top of a hill.

Most of the eight persons attending appear to be leaders of separate work groups that belong to Production Team No. 3, plus some cadres charged with specific tasks.

144

The main issue to be discussed is the nomination of candidates for the representative body of Emei district, as a preparatory step for the election of the National Congress. According to the Constitution every citizen may participate indirectly in the election of Congress members. Emei district is one of the 66 administrative units throughout China where, as an experiment, the local people can directly elect representatives up to the district level. The commune is organizing these preliminary elections.

The team leader, who chairs the meeting, starts by reading aloud the nomination requirements. A total of 14 candidates may be nominated by Longchi commune, 10 of which must be members of the Communist Party so as to ensure Party leadership. Five candidates should be proposed to represent different branches of production (industry, agriculture); cadres, including those at the commune level, can be nominated; workers in education, culture and health must also be taken into account. Nine candidates should represent peasants. In addition, candidates can be nominated simply as "citizens" and for each vacancy more than one candidate may be nominated.

An older man takes the floor and proposes a person who is always conscientious about his work and, despite his advanced age, works well.

Another older man proposes a commune cadre on the grounds that he unites with the mass of the peasants and applies the mass line well.

A younger speaker proposes a cadre from the subdistrict who has been shown to have a good mentality. Further, he proposes a barefoot doctor. As cadre from the commune level he proposes the Vice-Chairman of the Revolutionary Committee, a middle-aged man. "Since he has been working in the commune", he says, "he has always been honest".

Three women are proposed: the President of the Women's Federation in the subdistrict; an older woman, who belongs to Taoyuan brigade and a female teacher.

The first speaker observes that he does not know the commune cadres well; he finds it difficult to evaluate them.

During this discussion the Chairman, who takes notes, does not interfere. He then raises a second subject: the norms to be fixed for the production of winter wheat, and particularly the cultivation methods to be applied. The work has to be performed by two work groups.

The first speaker recommends close planting, in order to achieve a higher yield. This year there is a surfeit of water, owing to excessive rains. He proposes to deepen the ditches on the slopes, in order to improve drainage of the terraced rice fields.

He also proposes to consult the peasant masses on the planning of wheat cultivation. "We should apply all kinds of improvements". He counts upon surpassing the norm of 15,000 *jin* for the total production of winter wheat but to achieve this, chemical fertilizer should be used. This year's yield was 300 *jin* per *mou*, which was not bad, however, we should not be satisfied with it.

They had to seize the right moment to select the right seeds before the winter.

Another participant agrees that water drainage is the main task; only then will fertilizer be kept in the soil.

The first speaker urges everyone to express his opinion.

A young person says that he agrees with the two former speakers.

The older man who had earlier invoked the mass line suggests a certain amount of chemical fertilizer be used as a basis; afterwards, it can be supplemented if necessary. He also stresses the prevention of pests to safeguard the crops. Another speaker agrees.

The first speaker argues that a good method of planting is not enough; good management is also very important even if planting was satisfactory, a good harvest requires good maintenance. The management of the maize crop was good, and this accounts for the good harvest. (He points toward the full maize ears hanging in the granary.)

The cadres have to work with the idea of collective interests in mind. *We* are the "brains" of the masses. Good work depends on us; we have to become *good* leaders.

The Chairman, who so far has not intervened in the discussion, now starts summing up:

The winter wheat crop of 1978/1979 was 10,000 *jin*. Now, for 1979/1980, the expectation was 15,000. In order to achieve this, the following measures should be taken:

1. Drainage must be improved. This means that ditches will have to be dug. The preparation of chemical fertilizer has to be done diligently;
2. Close planting has already been applied, but not yet in the right manner. For the current year on each row of one meter 8 to 10 grains of wheat should be planted.

The first speaker adds that they, as cadres, have to demonstrate this method to the masses. They would need 30,000 plants per *mou*. Those present at the meeting should have a clear picture of the system.

The Chairman continues: as for chemical fertilizer first nitrogenous matter and later on matter containing potassium should be applied. This was important to guarantee good growth.

So far mainly one type of insecticide has been used. This year's wheat had been somewhat affected by insects. Precautions must now be taken.

The first speaker suggests a mixture of two kinds of oil, one derived from coal that is abundant in this area. This system might reduce production costs. All families should be mobilized to produce the oil mixture. According to the first experiments, it would also be effective to combat the rice-stem-borer.

This idea creates surprise among those present and immediately elicits a heated debate, in which also some of the provincial and district cadres who accompany us participate. The idea is evidently being supported.

Thus the gathering comes to a close. At a next gathering, which will be held in five days, on 18 October, the norms for a work day will be established, including remuneration and sanctions for not fulfilling the norms.

Stiefel observes that no decisions have been taken. How will they proceed in order to implement the plans? The answer is that only preliminary ideas were discussed. These will now be discussed among the masses. Then a new discussion of the cadres will be held where clear decisions that can be put into practice will be taken.

We inquire whether such gatherings of cadres are held regularly each week. This appears not to be the case; their meetings are always held at the start of some specific task to be performed. Team members are then convened to discuss the different points.

We ask why three persons have remained silent all the time. It appears that two of them are not actually engaged in production: one was the guardian of the granary; another was the responsible bookkeeper, who is also entrusted with calculating the distribution of work points among the team members.

The first, aged, speaker who gives the impression of being an extraordinary man full of ideas, appears to have been the sub-chief of the production team. (As in brigade No.1 of Liangjiafan, it seems that the *sub-chief* acts as the actual leader in the discussion, whereas the Chairman mostly contents himself with drawing conclusions.)

The other elderly speaker appears to be a party member who, as such, is always present at these meetings. He was the only one who expressed himself in more or less ideological terminology (for example, by referring to "the mass line"). The other participants were leaders of the different work groups.

We then ask what will be done about the candidates nominated for the District Congress. It appears that a meeting will be convened of all the Team members, at which names of the candidates to be forwarded to the commune (via the brigade) will be agreed. The brigade does not then make a selection but a list of candidates proposed by the different Teams, which goes to the commune administration. It may contain over 100 names (several names will appear on more than one list). The commune will publish all the names of candidates and return the list to the brigades, which will forward them to the Teams for further discussion, the results of which go back to the brigade.

In the consultation among the different brigades the list is then abridged to 28 persons. From these 28 the 14 definitive representatives are elected. Within the commune everyone over 18 years is entitled to participate in the elections.

The system of nomination for the Congress is a new one, based on the Constitution of 1978.

APPENDIX II

Production Plan and Projections for 1979 of Longmian Brigade, Tuyuan Commune, Xinhui County, Guangdong Province

The following production plan and economic projections give a rather good idea of how a brigade economy, that has been made unit of account, functions. It shows how production, costs and incomes are calculated, how income is distributed among taxes, savings, and brigade members, and how the value of a work point in agriculture, industry and the brigade as a whole is calculated.

1 *mou*:   1/15 ha.
1 *jin*:   1/2 kg.

龙眠大队一九七九年一年早知道

东风浩荡艳阳天，迎春花开尽娇妍。

战斗的一九七八年胜利地过去了，迎来了光辉灿烂的一九七九年，新的光荣而艰巨的一年又到来，特别是党的十一届三中全会公报发表以后全国形势一派大好，粉碎"四人帮"，抓纲治国，拨乱反正各项政策得到充分的落实，工农业生产热气腾腾，景象一片欣欣向荣。

当前"全党的工作着重点转移到社会主义现代化建设上来"这是关系到党和国家的前途和命运的大事，真是人心大快！我们大队受到极大鼓舞，有信心有决心把农业尽快搞上去"以粮为纲，全面发展"因地制宜适当集中为方针。根据公社党委提出的生产布局，经过研究讨论，联系实际，制订出我们的农，工副业的生产布局另粮食现金分配方案，按排如下，仅供全大队一千四百多名社员们参考。(总面积是1011⁵亩)

一、粮食收入与分配，布局，早造种水稻560亩，晚造种水稻750亩

（1）早造560亩，亩产要求610斤总产可达341600斤，亩种子14225斤，亩饲料粮4%是13396斤，上交公粮完成60%是60436斤，分口粮5个月277966斤欠缺喂24023斤，用花生1和3模谷解决。

（2）晚造750亩，亩产要求566斤，总产424500斤，亩种子11250斤，亩饲料粮16915斤，交公粮40363斤（免购转），分口粮七个月每人每月36斤阴粮351036斤，余5366斤。

二、花生收入与分配，布局，早造春花生252²⁄₃亩，晚造秋植花生87亩（已拓大面积70亩）

（1）早造花生252²⁄₃亩，亩产220斤总产55550斤，亩种子2621斤，上调国家10009斤，人口安化生每人每月吃1斤共24516斤，合计37146⁸⁄₉斤，剩余18403²⁄₃斤 解决早造口粮

三、现金分配，农业收入20万元，工副业收入25万元，争取双千30万元，农业工副业合计收入45万元，贵牧款积累，成本开支等社员分配平均每人126⁵⁵元，平均每请24⁰元，平均每户522元，展望新年到来，光明所在 同志们，努力奋斗吧！

LONGMIAN BRIGADE 1979 PROJECTIONS (translation)

The east wind brings a brilliant sky: flowers open to greet the Spring.

1978 is over, 1979 is upon us, bringing with it new struggles and new glories. The situation after the Third Plenary of the 11th Party Congress is excellent. The "Gang of Four" has been smashed and the country is moving from anarchy back to order. A new policy is being put into practice. Industry and agriculture are bursting with energy, looking forward to bright prospects.

The Party has decided to make socialist modernization its primary task, which will have tremendous impact on the future of our Party and our nation. Our brigade is impelled to greater efforts with confidence and determination. We are taking grain production as our key and at the same time striving for all-round development. We have considered our specific conditions and at the same time the need for appropriate centralization. Using as our basis the overall production plan of the Commune Party Committee, tailored to our own realities. We have discussed and consulted extensively among ourselves and are proposing to the 1,400 and some members of our Brigade the following projections for agricultural, industrial and subsidiary productions and plans for the distribution of grain and cash. Our total area under cultivation is 1011.5 mou.

- Grain Crops Production and Distribution: Cultivation pattern: rice 560 mou; late rice 750 mou.

(1) Early planting: 560 mou; yield expected: 610 jin/mou; total yield expected: 341,600 jin; retained for seeding: 14,225 jin; retained for feeds: 4% equivalent to 13,396 jin; contribution to state (60% of quota fulfilled): 60,436 jin; grain distribution among Brigade members (40 jin per person per month for five months): 277,966 jin; shortage: 24,023 jin made up by exchanging peanuts for grain at 1:3 ratio.

(2) Late planting 750 mou; yield expected 566 jin/mou; total yield expected 424,500 jin; retained for seeding 11,250 jin; for feeds 16,915 jin; contribution to state 40,363 jin (annual quota fulfilled); distribution among members (36 jin per person per month for seven months): 351,036 jin; net surplus: 5,366 jin.

= Peanuts Production and Distribution: Cultivation pattern: spring-planted peanuts 252.5 mou; autumn-planted peanuts 87 mou (including cultivated with expansion: 70 mou).

(1) Spring peanuts 252.5 mou; yield 220 jin/mou; total yield 55,550 jin; retained for seeding 2,621 jin; contribution to state: 10,009 jin; consumption by Brigade members (1.45 jin per person per month): 24,516 jin; grand total 37,146.8 jin; surplus 18,403.2 jin exchanged to make up for grain shortage.

= Cash Distribution: Revenue from agriculture 200,000 yuan; revenue from industry and sideline production 250,000 yuan (aiming for a target of 300,000 yuan); total income 450,000 yuan; after deducting taxes, savings, cost and expenses, average income distribution per person: 126,00 yuan; average income per labourer: 244 yuan; average income per family: 522 yuan. Comrades struggle hard and look forward to a bright new year.

153

一九七九年企业生产计划表

项目	人数	下达任务		全年总收入	计划成本		纯收入	收益分配	
		每人每天	全月		%	总成本		项目	金额
竹厂	63	2.50	4250.00	102000.00	50	51000.00	51000.00	总收入	227332
粮油	5	2.00	270.00	4628.00	30	1388.00	3240.00	总支出	94916
砂组	8	7.00	1512.00	36288.00	50	18144.00	18144.00	%	41.8
坭坊	12	2.50	810.00	12150.00	20	2430.00	9720.00	纯收入	132415
碓厂	21	3.00	1701.00	25515.00	20	5103.00	20412.00	%	58.2
数养	3	3.10	251.10	8180.20	60	5167.00	3013.00	税款	5000
溪坊	5	1.30		2730.00	30	630.00	2100.00	积累公积	22733
木组	2	1.32	71.28	881.80	3	26.44	855	%	10
理发	1	1.20	32.40	400.80	3	12.00	388.00	社员分配	104682
五金	6	3.50	566.00	13600.00	50	6800.00	6800.00	%	46
管理	1	1.50	40.50	555.40	30	69.00	486.00	企业工分	710000
农机	4	2.00		5184.00	50	2592.00	2592.00	工值	147
杀工业农	30	1.20		13219.00	25	1555.00	11664.00	全大队工分	3100000
竹园	4			2000.00			2000.00	工值	034
								平均社得分	634
				227332.20	41.80	94916.84	132415.36		

1979 ENTERPRISE PRODUCTION PLAN (Translation)

Items/ Enterprises	No. of persons engaged	Work perfmd. in yuan val. 1 per. 1 day	Value per month	Total annual revenue (yuan)	Projected cost %	Total cost (yuan)	Net Income (yuan)	Income distribution Items	Value in yuan
Bamboo factory	63	2.50	4,250.00	102,000.00	50	51,000.00	51,000.00	Total revenue	227,332
Oils	5	2.00	270.00	4,628.00	30	1,388.00	3,240.00	Total expenses	94,916
Sand-winnowing team	8	7.00	1,512.00	36,288.00	50	18,144.00	18,144.00	%	41.8
Brickyard	12	2.50	810.00	12,150.00	20	2,430.00	9,720.00	Net income	132,415
Brick-firing kiln	21	3.00	1,701.00	25,515.00	20	5,103.00	20,412.00	%	58.2
Tobacco processing	3	3.10	251.10	8,180.20	60	5,167.00	3,013.20	Taxes	@ 2.2% 5,000
Fishery	5	1.30		2,730.00	30	630.00	2,100.00	Savings	22,733
Carpentry	2	1.32	71.28	881.80	3	26.44	855.36	%	10
Barbershop	1	1.20	32.40	400.80	3	12.00	388.80	Distrib. among brig. members	104,682
Hardware	6	3.50	566.66	13,600.00	50	6,800.00	6,800.00	%	46
Repairs	1	1.50	40.50	555.40	30	69.40	486.00	Enterprise work points	710,000
Agriculture machinery	4	2.00		5,184.00	50	2,592.00	2,592.00	Cash value per work point	1.47
Part time industrial Part time agric. labour	30	1.20		13,219.00	25	1,555.00	11,664.00	Brigade total work points in agriculture & enterprise	3100,000
Bamboo grove	4			2,000.00			2,000.00	Cash value per work point	0.34
								Av. distrib. per labourer	634
Total	165			227,332.20	41.80	94,916.84	132,415.36	Av. production value/ labourer	1,380.00

龙眠大队一九七九年农业生产计划总表

经营项目	收入部分				支出部分		纯收入	收益分配		
	面积	亩产	总产	金额	亩成本	总成本		项目	农业	工业金额
早稻	567	609	345303	33839.00	18.-	10206.00	23633.69	总收入	202673.00	430000
晚稻	750	566	424500	41601.-	18.-	13500.00	28101.00	总支出	94965	189881.00
红薯	257	200	51520	28836.-	24.-	6168.00	22668.00	%	46.8	44.2
小麦	420	210	88200	9702.00	18.00	7560.-	2142.00	纯收入	107708.00	240119.00
春花生	241	220	53020	13255.-	21.-	5061.00	8194.00	%	53.2	55.8
秋花生	87	200	17400	4350.-	21.-	1827.00	2525.00	税款	9000	14000
番薯	54	2000	108.000	2700.00	8.-	432	2268.00	%	4.3	3.3
夏瓜	46	215.-		9890.00	73.-	1569.00	8321.-	积累合计	20267.00	43000
秋瓜	46	215.00		9890.00	73.-	1569.00	8321.-	%	10	10
香料作物	75	215.00		16125.-	73.00	5475.00	10650.00	社员分配	78441.00	183.119.00
冬种绿肥	23.5	215.-		5052.55	73.-	1715.00	3337.00	%	38.9	42.5
其他作物				11432.00		7094.00	4338.00	工分	240万	310万
牲畜				16000.00		16000.00		工值	0.34	0.59
什项						15000.00		平均每人	54.00	126.-
合计				202673.-		94965.-	107708.-	平均每劳	104.-	244.-

156

Items produced	R E V E N U E				Expenses		Net Income	INCOME DISTRIBUTION		
	Cult. area (mou)	yield (j/m)	Total yield (jin)	Value (yuan)	Cost/mou (yuan)	Total cost (yuan)	(yuan)	Items	Agricul. rev. dist. (yuan)	Ag.& Ind. rev. dist. (yuan
Early rice	567	609	345,303	33,839.^{69}	18.^{00}	10,206.^{00}	23,633.^{69}	Tot. rev.	202,673.^{00}	430,000.^{00}
Late rice	750	566	424,500	41,601.^{00}	18.^{00}	13,500.^{00}	28,101.^{00}	Total expen.	94,965.^{00}	189,881.^{00}
Tobacco	257	200	51,520	28,836.^{00}	24.^{00}	6,168.^{00}	22,668.^{00}	%	46.8	44.2
Wheat	420	210	88,200	9,702.^{00}	18.^{00}	7,560.^{00}	2,142.^{00}	Net income	107,708.^{00}	240,119.^{00}
Spring peanuts	241	220	53,020	13,255.^{00}	21.^{00}	5,061.^{00}	8,194.^{00}	%	53.2	55.8
Autumn peanuts	87	200	17,400	4,350.^{00}	21.^{00}	1,827.^{00}	2,523.^{00}	Taxes	9,000.^{00}	14,000.^{00}
Sweet potatoes	54	2000	108,000	2,700.^{00}	8.^{00}	432.^{00}	2,268.^{00}	%	4.3	3.3
Summer melons & gourds	46	(yuan) 215.^{00}		9,890.^{00}	73.^{00}	1,569.^{00}	8,321.^{00}	savings	20,267.^{00}	43,000.^{00}
Winter melons & gourds	46	(yuan) 215.^{00}		9,890.^{00}	73.^{00}	1,569.^{00}	8,321.^{00}	%	10	10
Spring cultiv.	75 (yuan)	(yuan) 215.^{00}		16,125.^{00}	73.^{00}	5,475.^{00}	10,650.^{00}	dist. among brig. members	78,441.^{00}	183,119.^{00}
Winter gatherings.	23.^{15}	215.^{00}		5,052.^{50}	73.^{00}	1,715.^{00}	3,337.^{50}	%	38.9	42.5
Other crops				11,432.^{00}		7,094.^{00}	4.338.^{00}	work points	2.4mil.	3.1 mil.
Pigs				16,000.^{00}		16,000.^{00}		Cash value per work pt.	0.^{34}	0.^{59}
Misc.						15,000.^{00}		Average per person	54.^{00}	126.^{00}
Total				202,673.^{00}		94,965.^{00}	107,708.^{00}	Average per labour	104.^{00}	244.^{00}

APPENDIX III

MAPS

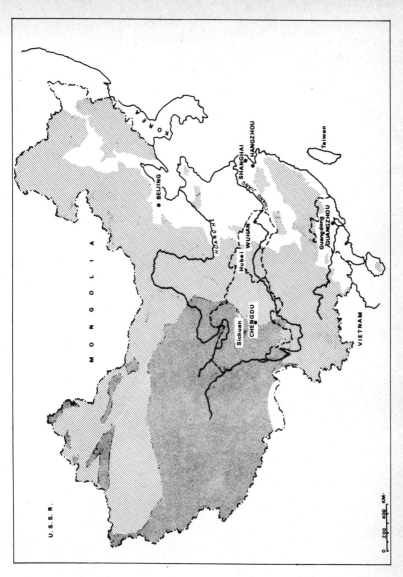

General map of the People's Republic of China, indicating major cities visited during the mission and the three provinces (Guangdon, Hubei, Sichuan) where field research was carried out.

161

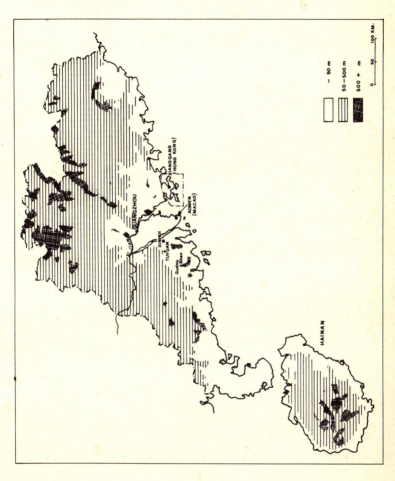

Map of the Province of Guangdong indicating Tuyuan commune (Xinhui county)

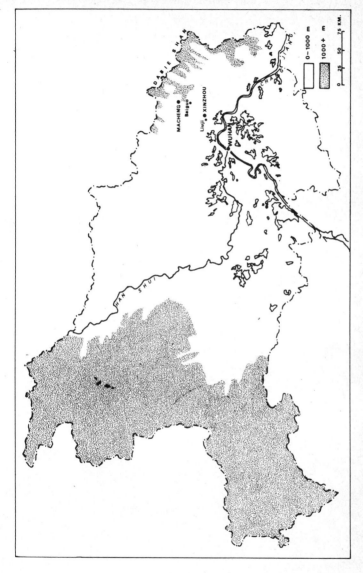

Map of the Province of Hubei, indicating Baiguo commune (Macheng county) and Liuji
commune (Xinzhou county). Liangjiafan subcommune is part of Baiguo commune.

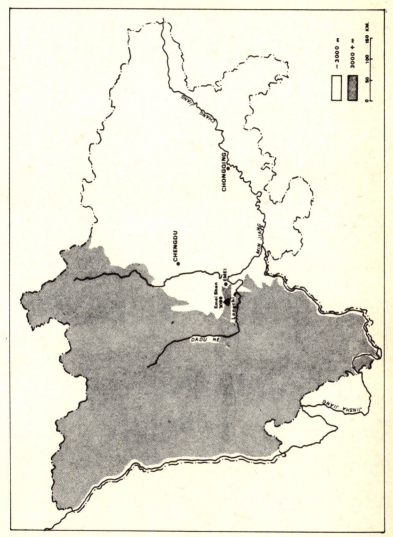

Map of Sichuan Province indicating Longchi commune (Emei county)

167

PUBLICATIONS

The following publications are now available in the Popular Participation Programme's Occasional Papers series:

* *Debaters' Comments on "Inquiry into Participation: A Research Approach" by Andrew Pearse and Matthias Stiefel*, compiled and edited by Selina Cohen, Geneva, 1981.

* *Some Dimensions of People's Participation in the Bhoomi Sena Movement: Followed by a Discussion on the Issue*, by Md. Anisur Rahman, Geneva, 1981.

  Algunos Aspectos de la Participación Popular en el Movimiento Bhoomi Sena: Seguido de una discusión sobre el tema, by Md. Anisur Rahman, Geneva, 1981.

* *Worker Participation in Company Management in Chile: A Historical Experience*, by Manuel Barrera, Geneva, 1981.

  La Participación de los Trabajadores en la Gestión de las Empresas en Chile: Una Experiencia Histórica, by Manuel Barrera, Geneva, 1981.

* *The Social Organization of Plantation Mackenzie: An Account of Life in the Guyana Mining Enterprises*, by Odida T. Quamina, Geneva, 1981.

  La Organización Social de la Plantación Mackenzie: Un Relato sobre la Vida en los Empresas Mineras de Guyana, by Odida T. Quamina, Geneva, 1981.

Dialogue about Participation 1, Geneva, June, 1981.
Diálogo sobre la Participación 1, Geneva, June 1981.

Dialogue about Participation 2, Geneva, April 1982.
Diálogo sobre la Participación 2, Geneva, April 1982.

Index

agriculture:
  diversification 32-4,66
  mechanization 22-4,41,69-70,79-80

Agricultural Bank of China 51-2

agricultural collectives: remuneration 44-7

Chinese:
  development: dialectical unity 132-4
                & South and Southeast Asia, compared 127-8
                diversity and complexity 127

communes: see also Cultural Revolution
  armed clashes 111
  Dazhai, as model 52-6
  income/distribution 47-9,56-60,63-9,74-6
  productivity 17-18,28-31,34-9

Cultural Revolution:
  & communes: authority structure 91-5
  effects 129-30

economic strategy:
  and over-population 14-20
  transition to per capita production 22-34,39-41

economic unequality: encouraged 56-60

Gang of Four: influences 103-4,107-8

family planning policies 13-14,18-19,20-22,25,35-9,120-21

investment-vs-living standards 68-9

industrial development 41

legal provisions 101-3

mass organizations: function 86

mass participation:
  the 'Democratic Wall' 101-2
  developments and trends 95-101
  disruptive developments 119-121
  general conclusions 134-7
  & the Party 83-4,104-111,121-5
  principles: democratic centralism/mass line 86-90
  reassessed 97-101

171

over-population:
  labour migration 14-15,26
  policy see family planning
  & underemployment 9-13

rural industry 26-7,39,76

scope and method of study 1-8

social welfare/state assistance 50-2,66-7,72,78-9,81

state farms: remuneration 52

taxation 49,68

'unit of account':
  deviations/effects 61-74,119
  structure/function 47,61

work points system 44-5,52,63

ASIA TITLES FROM ZED PRESS

POLITICAL ECONOMY

BEN KIERNAN AND CHANTHOU BOUA
Peasants and Politics in Kampuchea, 1942-1981
Hb and Pb

DAVID SELBOURNE
Through the Indian Looking Glass
Pb

HASSAN GARDEZI AND JAMIL RASHID (EDITORS)
Pakistan: The Roots of Dictatorship
The Political Economy of a Praetorian State
Hb and Pb

STEFAN DE VYLDER
Agriculture in Chains
Bangladesh — A Case Study in Contradictions and Constraints
Hb

REHMAN SOBHAN AND MUZAFFER AHMAD
Public Enterprise in an Intermediate Regime:
A Study in the Political Economy of Bangladesh
Hb

SATCHI PONNAMBALAM
Dependent Capitalism in Crisis:
The Sri Lankan Economy, 1948-1980
Hb

DAVID ELLIOT
Thailand: Origins of Military Rule
Hb and Pb

A. RUDRA, T. SHANIN AND J. BANAJI ET AL.
Studies in the Development of Capitalism in India
Hb and Pb

BULLETIN OF CONCERNED ASIAN SCHOLARS
China: From Mao to Deng
The Politics and Economics of Socialist Development
Hb and Pb

ELISABETH CROLL
The Family Rice Bowl
Food and the Domestic Economy in China
Hb and Pb

W.F. WERTHEIM AND MATTHIAS STIEFEL
Production, Equality and Participation in Rural China
Pb

CONTEMPORARY HISTORY/REVOLUTIONARY STRUGGLES

SUMANTA BANERJEE
India's Simmering Revolution:
The Naxalite Uprising
Pb

WILFRED BURCHETT
The China, Cambodia, Vietnam Triangle
Pb

SELIG HARRISON
In Afghanistan's Shadow:
Baluch Nationalism and Soviet Temptation
Hb and Pb

MUSIMGRAFIK
Where Monsoons Meet:
History of Malaya
Pb

LAWRENCE LIFSCHULTZ
Bangladesh: The Unfinished Revolution
Pb

HUMAN RIGHTS

PERMANENT PEOPLE'S TRIBUNAL
Philippines: Repression and Resistance
Pb

JULIE SOUTHWOOD AND PATRICK FLANAGAN
Indonesia: Law, Propaganda and Terror
Hb and Pb

WOMEN

BOBBY SIU
Women of China:
Imperialism and Women's Resistance, 1900–1949
Hb and Pb

ELSE SKJONSBERG
A Special Caste?
Tamil Women in Sri Lanka
Pb

GAIL OMVEDT
We Will Smash this Prison!
Indian Women in Struggle
Hb and Pb

AGNES SMEDLEY
Portraits of Chinese Women in Revolution
Pb

MARIA MIES
The Lacemakers of Narsapur:
Indian Housewives Produce for the World Market
Pb

PATRICIA JEFFREY
Frogs in a Well:
Indian Women in Purdah
Hb and Pb

Zed press titles cover Africa, Asia, Latin America and the Middle East, as well
as general issues affecting the Third World's relations with the rest of the
world. Our Series embrace: Imperialism, Women, Political Economy, History,
Labour, Voices of Struggle, Human Rights and other areas pertinent to the
Third World.

You can order Zed titles direct from Zed Press, 57 Caledonian
Road, London, N1 9DN, U.K.

NF

PT 80   136